9.00

ENDURING POLES

ENDURING POLES

By

NATSOLIM

MASSPAC Publishing Company
48855 North Gratiot Avenue
Mount Clemens, Michigan 48045

ISBN 0-918020-01-8 Hardbound $7.95
ISBN 0-918020-02-6 Softbound $4.95
Library of Congress Catalog Card Number: 76-42844

MASSPAC PUBLISHING COMPANY
48855 North Gratiot Avenue
Mount Clemens, Michigan 48045

Published 1977

Printed in the United States of America by
LithoCrafters, Inc., Ann Arbor, Michigan

This book was composed in IBM Press Roman with Globe Gothic Bold

CONTENTS

PREFACE

This book, *Enduring Poles*, is dedicated to the people of Slavic Extraction. The Slavic groups consist of the Slovene, Serbo-Croatian, Macedonian, Bulgarian, Czech, Slovak, Polish, Kashubian, Wendish, Polobian, Russian, Ukrainian, and the Belorussian peoples. Even though their neighbors speak the Baltic language, the Lithuanians and the Latvians at many times throughout history have been considered Slavic.

The Slavs, composing the bulk of the Caucasian branch, have suffered greatly, physically and psychologically because Slavic people are not demanding. Such virtue of non-demanding gave them endurance, hence the reason for the Slavs being in greater proportion in the world's population than any other stock of the white race.

In existence since pre-recorded history, this Endurance is possibly an Oriental trait.

This Endurance, if combined with the demanding factor of the non-Slavs, and very prevalent in America, could produce in the future either benign leaders or frightful despots. It is hopeful that these factors produce quickly what is needed—acceptable leaders.

As the Slavic people were never demanding in the Great Lakes Region, nothing has been written about this hard-working group. With that in mind, this book was written, and such book has long been overdue.

It is impossible to encompass all divergent Slavs but the various Slavs who contributed and produced in the Great Lakes Region are in this book.

This book is documentated, where stated, with authentic sources. Any person wishing to pursue in detail any persons(s), group, etc., can immediately go to the source as quoted to expound in detail their choice from any of the various chapters.

Possessing this endurance, any Slavic person will understand the humor, either subtle or in the inferred depth thought, that is in this book, along with the mythology, heritage and folklore (fact and fiction).

For the non-Slavic mind this book will explain the temperament and personality of the hard-working, proud, law-abiding and humorous Slavic people in the Great Lakes area. Arriving in 1820, then the Poles known as the "Novembrists" in 1834, and then in masses in 1854. Canada is included, as many came through Canada and some returned to Canada.

To the Slavic people who have assimilated into society by a change of name, Anglicizing their names or inheriting a name that is bilingual, or any of them who Americanized their name, remember that endurance is a virtue, which virtue is a genetic trait, so be boastful of this trait, *ENDURANCE*.

To the archivists, county clerks, record keepers, librarians, authors, proof readers, typists, critiques and friends—let them be thanked for their endurance. Without their help, the quoted records, etc., would still be lying dormant.

1
THE WHITE EAGLES ABDICATE GNIEZNO, POLAND

In the year of 1769 all the forestry students attending the colleges and universities in the vicinity of Gniezno, Poland, would venture out into the majestic forest. In the latter part of March, as part of their curriculum, the students would evaluate the damage done by the winter storms. At the same time, these forestry students were very ecologically minded and would make a computation of all the various new nests of the hawks and eagles, especially the white eagle. When these forestry students returned on Saturday, April 1, 1769, they all reported that the white eagles had no eaglets in their nests.

The great university minds, the foresters, and the other scholars of the time could not determine what caused the white eagles not to have any eaglets, so the mystery remained unsolved.

Their answer came in 1772 when all the white eagles flew to the North, or as it was then known in Poland, *do Pomorze*. The flight to the North was the last time the white eagles were in Poland, abdicating their majestic forests.

A person wonders why the white eagles left Poland in 1772. Was it that these eagles knew of the outcome of what was going to happen to their beloved people, that is, the Polish people around the ancient town of Gniezno?

A person only has to look at the history of Poland to recall that in the year 1772 occurred the first dismemberment of Poland, which was agreed upon between Russia, Prussia, and

Austria. It has been stated that Frederick the Great was the culprit who originated the idea of taking away Poland by partitioning. Possibly the eagles knew of the plundering which was to happen in their country, and such plundering was acquiesced by the Diet held at *Grodno*. At about the same time in Great Poland they were suppressing the Jesuits (to eliminate education). The politics went beyond any cure by the "gangrene" that they caused. Many of the people betrayed their own country for personal advantage. Who betrayed such country? Was it the so-called noble criminals, that is, were the noblemen actually criminals?

It is known that that was the beginning of the end of the great Polish democratic constitution, the end of true patriotism and dignity of its own people. Was this the downfall, could it be called the *TE DEUM*, which the eagles sang as they were flying North toward the Baltic Sea?

At this time of history nobody received credit for self-sacrifice. The foreign powers had endeavored in bribery of the Great Poland. The subsequent military leaders were not eligible for honor and trust. Much of the writing of the different agreements was in the so-called 18th century vogue style. This 18th century vogue style was very vague and had dual meanings. At about the same time, the Polish people started emigrating to other European countries and some even to America, never returning to their native Poland. A lot of the new rules that were written were borrowed from foreign legislation, making it impossible for a native Pole to retain his beloved land to toil the soil.

This foreign legislation would not allow any diplomatic act by the Poles with any other foreign nation. They eliminated all of the judicial power, and the policy was directed by unscrupulous and incompetent members of the local legislation. A lot of this evasive writing was the cause of the active interference by the Prussians. The Prussians accomplished this by acquiring the remainder of Great Poland, and the

Prussians did at that time, as we call it, *"FINIS-POLONIA."* After the finish of Polonia, there was loss of liberty, total ruin of their native country to the dear Poles. About the same time a Polish military man, Tadeusz Kosciuszko, travelled to Paris to enroll in the corps of cadets. This was possibly due to Poland being cut off from all and any hope, even to the last extremity.

The people realized that the Prussians were eager for all the spoils and more. The Prussians eliminated all institutions, and the self-abiding law perished. This was further accomplished by the coming of the Prussian '*LANDRECHT*.' The Prussians encountered serious problems because the Polish people did not want to be Germanized. Trying to eliminate this Germanization, there was a failure of the patriotic movement which was called the Confederation of Bar. At the same time there was a destruction of the interesting historical and literary rules of the Polish people. The Poles, along with the Prussians, would not listen to a private or a thinking group called the Dissidents.

Another reason why the white eagles left, never to return to Poland, is what they possibly saw from the Polish heavenly skies in the year of 1765. Did they witness and see the terrible massacres of the Roman Catholics and the Jews by the Cossacks? Did these white eagles see that Poland could not free itself of foreigners, which they tried, and such foreigners sold out to the three foreign groups of Austria, Prussia, and Russia. Realizing this, the partitioners took advantage of the old Polish animosity that they had toward the Dissidents. Furthermore, these foreigners saw the weakness in Stanislaus' character. Did these eagles realize the annihilation of the independence of Poland?

With all of this account we can always say: "What was the reason for the fall of the GREAT KINGDOM OF POLAND?" will always be a favorite subject of Polish eulogy.

But the question remains: Will the white eagles of Poland

ever return to their original nest in Gniezno, Poland, or did they fly to America to join the Bald Eagle where freedom would reign?

2
INSURRECTIONIST IN MICHIGAN

Ludwik Wesolowski was a Second Lieutenant during the Polish Insurrection of 1830-31, according to the "*Almanock Historique ou Souvenir de l Emigration Polonaise*" written by Adolph Count Krosnowski and printed in Paris in 1837 (Archives, Polish Library, Paris, France).

Wesolowski was in Michigan in 1834 and settled in Mount Clemens where he was an engineer on the defunct Huron-Kalamazoo Canal and later elected to the then important position of County Surveyor.

During this period of history, the beginning of the 19th century, the Serbs, Greeks, Czechs, Italians, Irish, Wallons, and South American countries wanted liberation. The Poles wanted their liberty from the despotic Russians who partitioned their land with Austria and Prussia. This quest for liberty by the Poles led to the Insurrection.

Russian Grand Duke Constantine, Czar Nicholas I's brother, was in charge of the Grand Duchy of Warsaw, which is like appointing a Protestant Pope.

On the night of November 29, 1830, the Polish Insurrection commenced to free Poland from Russian rule. University students "ignited" the "torch for freedom," and the brilliant Wesolowski was among them. This revolution was a regular war and was fought throughout that area of Poland.

The aged Lafayette spoke for Polish freedom, but Austria and Prussia backed up Russia, so the Poles fought the war without any assistance from their so-called allies, such as England and France.

From the start the valiant Poles were very successful and for ten months challenged the huge Russian Empire with their logistically trained army and their Polish patriotism (Polish Literary Society, Paris, France).

In September 1831 the Russians encompassed beautiful Warsaw and the patriotic Poles withdrew to the West. All freedom was abolished, and the soldiers were exiled to Siberia (unless they escaped), as were over 50,000 Polish families (children, parents, educators, etc.). The Russian policy of genocide was enforced and executed against the helpless Poles.

The Polish exiles that escaped this genocide were then deported by Austria and Prussia, and then began the GREAT POLISH EMIGRATION to other free European and African countries, and of course the UNITED STATES OF AMERICA, Canada, and Central and South America.

The youthful Ludwik was informed that he would be sent to France, but the deceptive Chancellor Metternich had him thrown into prison where he received only enough food to sustain sanity, soul and body.

In the summer of 1833 Wesolowski was taken to the port of Trieste and told that he was being sent to America (almost 5,000 miles away), according to all accounts of this event.

At Trieste, Wesolowski, confined in prison, revolted against the Austrian policies. He then was allowed to visit the city under armed guard. He managed to mail letters of desperation and treatment received to some of his commanding officers in France.

Eventually, Ludwik was given an overcoat, a pair of pants and underwear, and embarked at Trieste early on the morning of November 22, 1833, either on the Austrian frigate *Hebe* or the other frigate *Guerriera*, under the command of Colonel (Captain) *Bandier* (Polish Library, Paris).

Chancellor Metternich's vague correspondence concerning these exiles, in his style of deception and double talk, equalled Secretary of State McLane's non-commital and evasive procrastination. The exiles wanted proof of the diplomatic agreement, but to this date such agreement has not been found.

The first part of the voyage to Gibraltar was horrendous. No winds in the Adriatic Sea and the Mediterranean. Contaminated water. Fighting with the Austrian crew which was miraculously halted. On February 14, 1834, the frigates with the captive exiles departed from Gibraltar and the Poles were placed under heavy guard (Polish Library, Paris).

Although completely exhausted and undernourished by the 42-day voyage from Gibraltar, the Polish exiles arrived in New York on the night of March 28, 1834, with enthusiasm, as now they were in America. These Polish exiles knew that Poland never allowed servitude, but after the ocean voyage, they experienced the "slave-ship" treatment as had other persons brought to these shores without their consent.

Metternich's deception was not eased when the Austrian Consul Baron Lederer gave Ludwik $33.00, and in essence said: "Ludwik, you are over 5,000 miles away from home and you are on your own," (translation from the records at the Polish Library in Paris).

Stepping ashore, Ludwik commenced looking for food and shelter. He found a boarding house where he paid $3.00 a week. No kielbasa, until the Polish boarders made their own, and the New York natives relished this new sausage, "*keel-bass-saw*," hence, the first Polish Delicatessen in America.

At twenty years of age, Ludwik was a leader of a war battle regiment fighting for freedom and liberty. On his 24th birthday he was in the middle of the treacherous Atlantic Ocean, with cracked ship decks, broken masts, bitter cold, and the gale winds of winter, heading for a country that accepted him.

The writer theorizes that Ludwik was one in the group that had knowledge of the English language, as he knew Polish, German, Latin, French, Russian, hence, a linguist also.

Wesolowski settled in the Village of Marcelles (now Mount Clemens), Michigan, where in 1838 he purchased a lot along the then Huron River (presently the Clinton River at Gratiot Avenue), as recorded in the Office of the Register of Deeds, Macomb County. He was employed as a draftsman on the Huron-Kalamazoo Canal, which canal was never finalized. Subsequently an engineer, then a surveyor, and after being naturalized in 1846 (discovered at the excellent records of the Macomb County Clerk's Office), he was elected County Surveyor under the Whig Party in 1850. In 1862, Ludwik was again elected under the Democratic Party, as County Surveyor.

Forty years after the Insurrection, Wesolowski could have been reminiscing about that first day of battle, when on November 20, 1870, Ludwik, who was then 60 years and 10 months old, died in Macomb County, as the engraving on his tombstone indicates.

With all the problems encountered in life, Wesolowski has been in perpetual peace since 1870, alongside his beloved wife, Sarah Jane, in Section A, lot 234 (six spaces), which Ludwik purchased in May 1860 when Sarah Jane died, in the beautiful Clinton Grove Cemetery, Mount Clemens.

The Insurrectionist found love, freedom, employment, political office, and liberty in a Michigan County that today is over 65% Slavic. Wesolowski was the first in Macomb County, and he set the trend for immigrants to settle in Macomb County.

3
POLSKA, MICHIGAN

The Insurrectionists, after their arrival in America, were promised by the Congress of the United States a section of land. A section of land constitutes 36 square miles.

From the archives of Poland and the United States, it is revealed that on September 9, 1834, three Polish people–namely, Jan Rychlicki, Edward Mlodzianowski, and a Michal Gorski–were part of a delegation that was assigned to investigate the prospects of obtaining a section of land in Michigan.

Rychlicki wrote from Detroit in part: "It seems to me that it will be rather difficult to choose Michigan as the place of our colonization. The best locations are occupied–although there is still no lack of good places for other purposes . . . The Americans are everywhere alike and it is difficult to set out on a journey without some funds. I myself do not know what will become of me as I am without a cent . . . If one does not have a definite destination at which one ultimately aims, it is better to remain in New York. There are swindlers and sharps all along the way; they strip you of your funds in an unheard of manner. Nearly everything here in Detroit is more expensive than in New York."

It is known that they ventured from Wyandotte to Port Huron, Michigan, as ship was the mode of transportation in 1834. It is further theorized that they were shipped up along the Huron River, which is presently the Clinton River in Macomb County. It is the theory of the writer that one who settled and was an engineer on the canal must have been in the group, and that is Ludwik Wesolowski.

The problem along the lake and river was that it was filled with squatters and other people who were in possession. Much of the land was granted as bounty land. There were other sections inland from the lake or river area but these were inacessible due to lack of transportation.

One often wonders if these Novembrists—who were all university educated in the fields of languages, engineering, and other subjects—would have settled in one section, then they would have been in a community that would have had the most educated persons in the State of Michigan.

4
THE HURON CANAL VANGUARD

Thirty-one years after its organization, the Michigan Territory, in 1836, was looking forward to becoming a State in the Great Union the following year, especially among the French in Detroit and surrounding areas.

A youthful Polish surveyor and draftsman, trained in military engineering and languages, arrived with a group of "Novembrists" during the summer of 1834, seeking farm and forest land along the water route from Detroit to Port Huron. Congress was to grant this group a section of land for the payment of the services of the Polish soldiers, including Generals Pulaski and Kosciusko, during the American Revolutionary War. The group, after traversing all of the land, decided that the best land had been taken or possessed by squatters. At Detroit, on September 9, 1834, their letter to the New York City Office stated that they were returning East, with the exception of the French and English speaking surveyor who liked Detroit with its French and Polish Pomeranian families.

Ludwik Wesolowski, age 24, spoke and read six languages fluently. He decided that the Michigan Territory would not suppress his challenging frontier spirit, so he remained in Detroit. Detroit was a bustle with Governor Cass and a Mr. Brush platting the farms for subdivisions and selling such lots to the newly arrived immigrants. Surveyors and draftsmen were in great demand, so young Wesolowski was immediately employed.

Ludwik spoke to the prominent French people about Detroit, even talking to Bishop Rese. Still single, he spoke to the Polish Pomeranian families. When Wesolowski got ducks and geese from French and Indian hunters and trappers, he was, of course, invited for *czarnina* dinners by the Polish families.

During 1835 Detroit was prospering. Ludwik wanted to perfect his skill. He again visited the French village of Belvidere, along the mouth of the present Clinton River, after the rumor of the Great Huron Canal was published in the newspapers. Revisiting the area this year, as he did in 1834 when scouting for farm and forest land with the Novembrists, he immediately contacted the French and Indian river guides, hunters and trappers. With their able assistance, Wesolowski scrutinized all of the Huron (presently Clinton) River and the river's numerous branches. Along the river route he saw the majestic oaks, maples, black walnuts and whitewood, mentally evaluating such timbers for construction of the canal.

Again in 1836, Wesolowski visited the Huron River area. Taking the secret information of all the visits, trips, surveys, etc., which he had written in the complicated Polish language, to the liaison men of the "Canal Operators," he immediately was retained as a draftsman for the world's "GREATEST" canal, that was to be built when Michigan obtained statehood.

In 1837 he settled in Belvidere, where he was gainfully employed, surveying and scouting the water route of the future canal. Then the depression struck Detroit, with the so-called "depreciated money of 1837" financially ruining Detroit for a few years.

The 26th State, organized in 1805 as a separate territory, was admitted to the Union on Thursday, January 26, 1837, and retained the Michigan territorial name. After statehood, the problem was transportation and water for expansion, a problem which the Michigan House of Representatives immediately placed on their agenda.

Succintly, the new State passed the following laws:

1. On the practicability of constructing a canal from Mount Clemens to Lake Michigan, in the County of Allegan.

2. The estimate of the engineer on sixty miles of the route in Macomb and Oakland Counties.

In a very convincing manner, the Commissioners of the Board of Internal Improvement said:

A. They decided said route to be practicable.

B. Canal can be constructed throughout the entire distance of Michigan.

C. Construction at a reasonable expenditure.

D. Said canal will provide an abundant supply of water procured at all seasons, and at a moderate expense.

E. There is a superior advantage of canals over railroads.

The commissioners added the estimate of the engineers for the first sixty miles, for calculating the locks, culverts, and aqueducts to be built of stone; and some locks of wood, and some locks with stone foundations and residue of wood. The total amount with timber locks from Mount Clemens to Oar Creek, a distance of 59 miles, is $658,020.29 (average per mile, $11,153.05); or 59 miles of other locks at $990,550.29, averaging $16,890.68 per mile.

The report to the annual session at Detroit, on February 27, 1839, reported the wages:

Chief engineer,	at	$1,800.00	per annum.
Draftsman. . . .	at	$1,000.00	per annum.
Rodman.	at	$32.50	per month, when working.
Chainman. . . .	at	$20.00	per month, when working.
Axman.	at	$18.00	per month, when working.

The engineer and draftsman were making out the plans, drawings, specifications, etc., for the locks, bridges, aqueducts, culverts, etc. "There are not more engineers employed on said work than the interest of the State requires," was said by the new acting Commissioner, in his conclusion, as the newly admitted state was being overflooded with skilled manpower from the eastern states and Europe.

The axmen earned $18.00 per month, for 12 hours per day, six days a week, so at 26 working days per month they earned about 70 cents per day or almost six cents per hour.

The draftsman had been educated in Poland, but because he was a Novembrist, he was not able to return to Russian-ruled Poland. So on July 10, 1838, he commenced building a home for his new bride in the Village of Marcelles, lot one, section eight, as recorded in the Macomb County Register of Deeds Office, Liber L, page 170. His earnings of $3.22 per day had enabled Wesolowski to purchase this lot on the south side of the Clinton River, east of the Gratiot Turnpike, for $30.00.

Having encountered financial problems, the acting Commissioner's report of February 12, 1841, stated:

1 principal engineer at only $1,000 per annum.

1 assistant engineer at only $800.00 per annum.

1 leveller at $60.00 per month, oxen self provided.

2 rodmen at $45.00 per month, and the 3 axmen at $30.00 per month, as they are only seasonal employees. Total amount paid for engineering on the Clinton and Kalamazoo Canal, from May 1, 1840, to January 31, 1841, including salaries of engineers, levellers, rodmen, and axmen, office rent, stationery, etc., etc., is reduced to $3,588.63.

The canal construction was ebbing, due to financial problems, pilfering by the unpaid contractors, embezzlement of the capital amount, so the dream passed into oblivion before 1845. Certain portions of the canal are still in existence.

The original draftsman, who was naturalized in April, 1846, at Mount Clemens, was later an assistant engineer on the canal project and realized the problems. He submitted his pleasant personality to the voters, and was elected Macomb County Surveyor, in the 1850 election, under the Whig Party candidacy. After two years in office, he platted villages, cities, and surveyed throughout southeastern Michigan and Lambton County, Canada. In the 1862 Civil War period, he was again elected surveyor under the new Democratic Party, while his assistant surveyor, son Albert, enlisted with the Mount Clemens Company F, 22nd Regiment, Michigan Infantry.

The surveyor's only daughter, Helena Jane Wesolowski, was born in 1845, at Pine and Market Street (church property presently), Village of Mount Clements, lot 9, section ten, as in Liber M, page 230. She was still in school after her sixteenth birthday, a rarity in the 1860's, The 5′5″ auburned-haired, hazel-eyed beauty was married at the age of 22, on Wednesday, July 10, 1867, to William H. McGarvey, a merchant from Petrolia, Ontario, in Mount Clemens, by Reverend H. E. Bissell. The Polish reception was held at Ludwik's 5.6 acre estate on North Avenue at Market Street (church property presently). Helena became the first Michigan multi-millionairess from oil operations in Canada, Austria, Galicia, and the world's largest oil refineries in Trieste. She died in December, 1897, in her mammoth castle, overlooking the canal locks at Port Gorlice, Galicia.

The retired surveyor only enjoyed his daughter's early wealth, as he died on November 20, 1870, at New Baltimore, Michigan. He is buried in the Mount Clemens Clinton Grove cemetery, on Cass Avenue, and since 1915, Section A, lot 234, has been maintained without a visit from a relative, friend, or voter. Nor did he expect at death that his vivacious glamorous granddaughter would become Countess Mamie Helena Graf von Zeppelin, at the most festive of the century's three-day wedding in Vienna, commencing on Thursday, November 12, 1896, alongside the banks of the then green 'waltzing' Blue Danube canal.

A few episodes of Wesolowski's fascinating life reveals that in his surveying of the present Anchor Bay area

Wesolowski would embark at the present foot of Cotton Road in Chesterfield Township, walk up the hill towards the Gratiot Turnpike, where near the huge tree of the eagle's nest lived an old French-speaking Chippewa Indian, Chief *Merle* (Blackbird, in English). Chief *Kos*, as Ludwik called him, always fed his friends with smoked *sledzie* (herring). After the feast, Chief Kos in jest would inform Ludwik that a reddish brown scalp would be a unique addition hanging inside the huge colorful wigwam. Ludwik did not smoke the peace pipe, as smoking was forbidden in his youth while attending a Polish university. In his witticism, Wesolowski countered with the Chief being "well done" by being "smoked internally."

Wesolowski also surveyed and platted the City of Warsaw, which is presently along Cass Avenue at the railroad tracks and depot, in Mount Clemens, Michigan. Speaking to everyone on his train rides from the Warsaw depot to Detroit, where Wesolowski visited the Pomeranians, Poznanians, Kashubians, and Silesians who emigrated to Michigan in masses in 1854, he encountered a hard-working teenager who always quizzed Ludwik about the variation and deviation of the compass, his education in Europe, and his many travels. The teenager, having an inquisitive scientific mind, listened as Wesolowski explained in detail the potential of water power, such as the canal project could provide, the future of transportation, and the theories of celestial bodies as Copernicus expounded. The youngster followed the advice of Wesolowski by quitting his job on the railroad. The youngster was Thomas Edison.

For a part of Michigan history, take a day's tour to explore the remaining evidence of the "world's greatest canal."

For a day's trip, start at the Mt. Clemens Library, on Cass Avenue, for history and information about the canal. Then proceed west on Cass Avenue to the railroad tracks and the old City of Warsaw depot. Continue west on Cass

Avenue to the Clinton Grove Cemetery. Go west again, crossing the Clinton River at the New Bridge, and turn on Canal Road. Along Canal Road observe the deep ditches that were part of the Canal. Follow Canal Road to Utica where you take Shelby Road where part of the canal meandered into the river. At 23 Mile Road, turn west and continue until the Cider Mill. Park at the cider mill, as in the back of the mill is a path alongside the old canal. Notice the rapid flow of the river below the canal. Across the road from the mill, take a photograph of the flow of the river bend from alongside the old canal where it flows into the river. Then proceed to Rochester.

THE 1838 CONSTRUCTED CANAL TODAY

Educated in engineering in Warsaw, Poland, Ludwik Wesolowski was an engineer which constructed the Huron-Kalamazoo Canal. To this date part of the canal is very evident in Macomb County, Michigan.

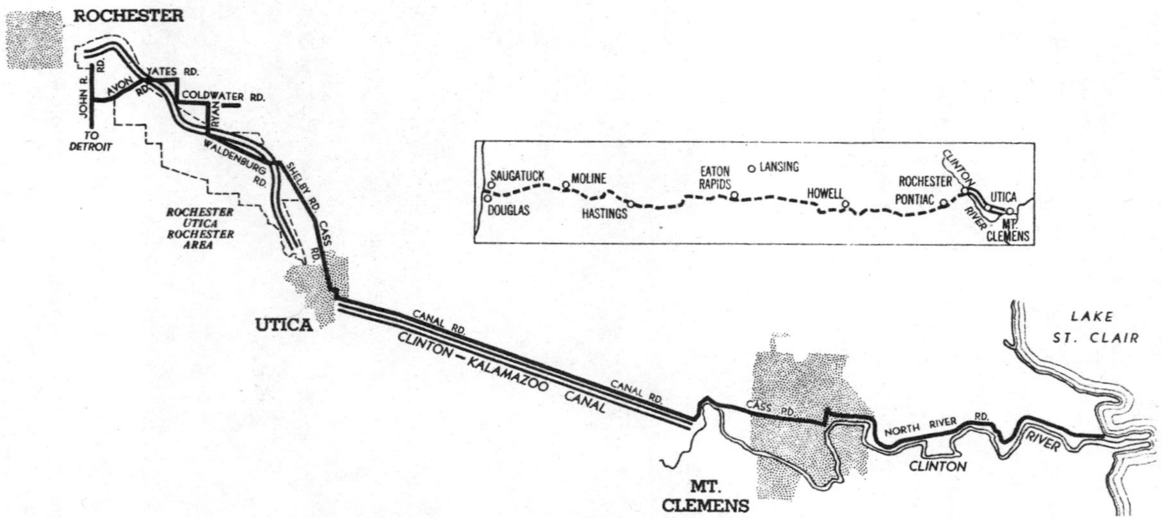

THE "GREATEST" CANAL IN THE WORLD?

The inset reveals that the Huron-Kalamazoo Canal would start at Lake St. Clair, then to Pontiac, Howell, Eaton Rapids, Hastings, Saugatuck and then into Lake Michigan. Work on the canal commenced in 1838, ended at Rochester in 1843.

The Polish engineer, Ludwik Wesolowski, surveyed the project and was employed on this canal until 1843.

Wesolowski received his university education in Warsaw, Poland. An insurrectionist of 1830, he was deported by Austria in 1833. He was in Michigan during the summer of 1834 scouting for the section of land that Congress promised to the Poles.

5
THE PHENOMENON OF THUNDER BAY

At the Bentley Historical Library, Ann Arbor, Michigan, under the heading of Macomb County, are the field notes of a Bela Hubbard, who along with his wife Mrs. Hubbard, made a peninsular coast survey during the year 1838.

Thunder Bay was mentioned, and on June 13, 1838, Bela Hubbard made many notes. Here are a few of the excerpts from his notes.

Hubbard stated as he approached Thunder Bay from the southeastern point at the shore he found it to be about a fathom deep and the limestone was lying with fragments of lines. Upon examination he found it to be petrification and one of the stones he noted was encrinite. He collected numerous specimens of the various stones including the tribolite. He also stated there were indications of slate.

Hubbard stated he dined at this point and paddled across toward Thunder Bay River and the north wind was blowing strongly into this bay from the east northeast direction.

He continued by stating this whole bay is very shoal, the bottom appearing in many places and at times there are boulders. As he approached the mouth of the river he noticed that there was a heavy standing of cedar. From the present position at the mouth of the Thunder Bay River and looking south there was a group of hills which appeared to be of a mountainous aspect through that south region. He stated that possibly the opposite inclination of the rocks was the result of what is called an uplift. Timber today was mostly pine, cedar, but much mixed with hardwood. The timber of the elevated ridges was pine.

He then ascended Thunder Bay River to the rapids which were 3/4 of a mile, and he stated the river was wide and deep. Along the river there were preparations that were being made which seemed to him to be the making for a mill, although they saw no white inhabitants. He further stated that such site could be more eligible for the purpose of a mill as the timber is white and Norway pine and some cedars which were uncommonly huge. The banks from the bay had an elevation of 30-35 feet and were of sand. The rapids were over limerock which is similar to that he examined in entering Thunder Bay. Some of the limerock had slate and shale and they appeared on the west side of the hills of the Thunder Bay River.

He then stated that "much mystery has been attached to this bay." From the time of the earliest voyages to the lakes the thunder was of frequent occurrence even with the clear sky. The fact was no doubt magnified in those early times, partly, perhaps, from the inclinations so common to wanderers in regions that were scarcely known to the white, hence to give an air of mysterious importance to the tales they have to reiterate.

Without stopping to examine the causes offered in explanation of the phenomenon, it is sufficient to say that thunder has been heard each day since leaving the area of Squaw Bay. Until today the weather has been changeable. Today was fair with the wind north and northeast. An explanation no doubt may be found in the form of the coast. For this bay, the coast lies in a southwestern part of the Saginaw Bay and a northwestern district to Mackinac. The meeting of winds from these two quarters would be attended by a condensation of warmer winds which might naturally give rise to the electrical phenomenon that was observed.

In his log for Thursday, June 14, 1838, Hubbard stated

that he was being detained by a head wind and a heavy surf and he could not leave until nine o'clock. They then were forced by heavy sea to make it to the southern shore where they remained at a point on the southern shore of Thunder Bay. That evening they camped at the southern shore and again a storm arose and it had been raining and the rain was accompanied with low mumbling scales of thunder and flashing of lightning until seven o'clock in the evening, at which time a cloud was heading off to the south direction. He noticed that the beach had many pebbles.

In that afternoon there was a change of wind and a constant thunderstorm which offers a solution to the phenomenon of Thunder Bay. With an easterly wind during the whole time of their camping in the bay until this p.m. they had weather that was clear and cloudy with the wind strong and later no thunder. Today, it is said in his book, we again experienced the natural result of the meeting of the northerly and southerly winds or a west wind making up a peculiar condensation of the coast and encountering each other at this point.

Friday, June 15, entry stated that the wind was southeast this morning and they embarked without breakfast and they rowed to the Thunder Bay Islands, a distance of three miles. They landed at eight o'clock at the lighthouse, claiming the shore was rocky. He stated he saw no landing place as he coasted along the northern shore and saw rock at the bottom. He stated the depth could not be ascertained. He then explained the color. It was a dark color similar to slate. Other stone that was a lighter color is harder and more crystalline.

He stated that a lighthouse has been erected here and the island appears to be an important fishing ground, but it has been but little frequented for that purpose until the last season (that is, 1837). He stated that there are now a dozen or more gill nets that are in operation, and last season about 600 barrels of whitefish were taken. Sturgeon are seldom taken in this way. The fish are principally whitefish and are large; some trout are also taken. He then went on to explain the various rocks and rock formation on the island.

He stated that there were two species of plants that were in flower at that time and were discovered on this island. One of the plants is a perennial herb which has basil leaves and has various colored flowers. The other plant is not known to Hubbard and would possibly be known to a botanist. He noticed that on that day on Thunder Bay Island "it was showery and warm all day with continued thunder and the wind from the southeast."

In his log dated Saturday, June 16, 1838, he commenced with the wind being southeast all day and fair. No rain or thunder. Cloudy part of the afternoon.

He remained on the island waiting for a boat to take Mrs. Hubbard and one S. Dunlap to Detroit. He also packed two casks of specimens. He stated that he conversed with a man who said he had walked a ridge from the Thunder Bay River to the AuSable. The man stated he saw no rock along the shore and the timber is primarily Norway pine and the country is sterile (sterile at that time meant without vegetation). This person further explained to Hubbard that he "observed a rock on the AuSable sixty miles up in a high ledge and in the bed of the stream."

Hubbard continues by stating at instance how much the configuration of this coast has been misconceived. "Surveying parties for the present were either ordered to make a certain number of certain lines and they were supposed to survey up to the middle island where presently they are thirty miles south from the point of the southeast point of Thunder Bay."

This person that conversed with Bela Hubbard stated

that "beaver and otter are still numerous in the regions of Thunder Bay and in sufficient numbers to make the fur business profitable but the Indians are too lazy to hunt much."

The recording for Monday morning, June 18, stated yesterday there was a mild wind from the southeast but shifted to the northwest toward the evening. There was an increase of the wind which brought fog and the fog lasted until the wind changed in the afternoon. This again occasioned thunder without rain and it dispersed the mist. This morning we again had fog. These fogs which we have experienced one half of the time of our stay on the island are so dense that a vessel would not be visible a few rods from the shore. Fishermen often lose themselves when near shore and wander a long time before making this port as this place in the fog is scarcely discernible.

Last night was foggy. The night before there was a fog until 3 a.m. We have kept watch day and night for a boat but have seen none except one from Detroit which a misty fog obscured just as she nearly made the island. We could not ascertain her name. Not a sail has appeared in the other direction unless under cover of the fog. This island contains three families and forty-six fishermen. He continued by stating the fog cleared up about 7 a.m., at which time we embarked, leaving Mr. Dunlap with the casks of specimens on the island to return to Detroit by the first opportunity.

He then stated that Mrs. Hubbard would accompany him on the way to Mackinac. The shore from Flat Rock to Little Thunder Bay appears to be sandy with occasional high banks. They stopped to examine the stones, and the stones were of lighter color than those of Thunder Bay Island. He again named the type of stones.

He continued by stating on approaching the point about three miles below Middle Island he saw rock on the bottom of the lake which was cropping out in ridges. The depth could not be ascertained. He continued by stating the rock is a gray color limestone of lighter color and more crystalline than that which was on Outer Thunder Bay Island and it is overlaid with a dark slate.

From that point he took across to Middle Island which was reached at 4 p.m. and they encamped on the west side of the island. He continued by stating that the northwest and west shores of this island, at least as far as can be seen, are lined with broken pieces of limestone which were much torn by water and along the whole a beautiful beach of pebbles of limestones. The banks were of an average of four to five feet in height. He then made an examination of the island for the various types of stone. And, of course, from this island he continued north to Mackinac Island with his wife, whose first name was not given.

In the sketch of these books is a picture of Bela Hubbard. He seems to be of a slim stature having a mustache and beard and in this sketch it was shown where he was making notes. Hubbard wore glasses, and had the Chippewa name of *MAS-CO-MA*, which is Red Wolf, possibly so named due to his red beard and hair.

This area of Thunder Bay and Thunder Bay Island was twice visited by Poles in 1834, when they were in the Great Lakes area searching for the 36 square miles of land that was promised to them. A colony was established in Illinois by the Polish Insurrectionists, under a grant by Congress.

Hubbard and his relatives resided in the then Village of Mount Clemens, Michigan. A neighbor across the road was Ludwik Wesolowski, who in 1838 purchased land in Macomb County, and is considered the first Pole who had his land recorded in the State of Michigan.

The phenomenon of Thunder Bay will continue to be a mystery to many person, especially persons who fear the sound of thunder. However, this mystery might be partially resolved by the readers of this chapter, especially the people who reside in that Thunder Bay area.

6
POLISH DINNER

The Poles are a very intersting people, and they have always been known for their good food.

The following information was taken from the Archives in Paris, France, which were eventually translated into English. This is a report of a visit to Poland by a French woman, who eventually became the Queen of Poland. She was accompanied on this visit to Poland by her governess, a Madame de Grubirant. This report was written by Le Labourex, secretary to Madame de Grubirant, and has been in the French Archives for over 330 years.

In sixteenth century Poland there was a rise of the middle class due to the development of the emancipation of the Polish peasant–such emancipation coming from the limitation of the power of the so-called aristocracy.

With the rise of the middle class, the quality of the food improved and it was served in courses. The appearance of the food pleased the eye extremely and appearance alone truly gave an appetite.

There was a number of spices in the food, but the main spices were saffron and sour salt. The sour salt was mined in Poland, the only part of the world that has such sour salt.

In his memoirs the secretary claimed that the sight of the food gave a better picture than Cana, and the dishes were always filled. Eggs and milk were very abundant, as was butter.

The paté consisted of either a fish or meat pie or patty. Another style of the paté was a spread of finely mashed seasoned and spiced meat and fish.

In the hall of their homes, which was similar to a banqueting hall, musicians played at one end, delighting the mind and the eye.

Some of the desserts were several candied fruits, sugared delicacies, and confectionaries.

When in season there were frozen dainties. There was a dish which was a favorite Lithuanian preparation called *cholodziec*, and the ingredients were: beet root leaves, cream, and fruit congealed. It is to be noted that this recipe went into oblivion and could never be resurrected.

The bread was cut in half, then a plate was filled with meat, and the first plate was given to the servant who ate with the family. (Democracy prevailed first in Poland).

There were several varieties of wine and other liquors. The other liquors were not named by the secretary.

There were also dry sweet meats–a food that was rich in sugar. The fruits in that period of history were crystallized fruits.

There were also various soups at these banquets, including czarnina which was made from either ducks or geese.

After a lengthy time in eating, the people in the home resorted to dancing. This was a Polish dinner for festivity in the year 1645 in Wielka Polska as recorded by the secretary.

A Polish proverb states that good and abundant food is required for good health. *LEPIEJ WYDAC DO PIEKARZA, NIZ NA APTEKARZA*.

This proverb is still visible in the kitchens of the Polish American people after seven generations in the Great Lakes area. With such good food, it is impossible to refuse an invitation to a Polish dinner!

7
FIRST POLISH PROPERTY OWNER IN MICHIGAN

The Macomb County residents, over one-half having Polish blood, can feel proud of home ownership, as the first recorded property owner of Polish lineage was Ludwik Wesolowski, who in fact was the first Pole to record the property purchase in the new State of Michigan.

Wesolowski was born in Warsaw on March 3, 1810, and educated at the Military Institute. On November 29, 1830, while still a student, he rebelled against the Czarist rule, and as a "Novembrist" he was deported by Austria from Trieste arriving in New York in 1834 with a $7.00 grant.

Trained in engineering and having knowledge of the English language, he ventured to Michigan and found employment as a draftsman on the Clinton and Kalamazoo Canal. Earning $3.22 per twelve hour day enabled Ludwik to purchase a lot on the south side of the Clinton River, east of the Gratiot Turnpike, for $30.00, where he commenced building a house on July 10, 1838, in the Village of Marcelles, lot one, section 8, as recorded in the Macomb County Register of Deeds Office, Liber L, page 170 (motel at present).

He was naturalized in 1846 at Mount Clemens, Michigan, where his wife Sarah Jane (nee Fletcher) was in attendance with their oldest son Albert, who later enlisted in the Army for the Civil War, and daugher, Helena Jane.

The original draftsman, later an assistant engineer of the canal project, realizing the canal financial problems in talking to all the residents of Macomb County, submitted his pleasant personality to the voters and was elected Macomb County surveyor in the 1850 election under the Whig Party candidacy. After two years in office, he platted villages, cities, and surveyed throughout southeastern Michigan and Lambton County, Canada. In the 1862 Civil War period he was again elected surveyor under the new Democratic Party and platted the City of Warsaw, Macomb County (Cass Avenue at the depot).

The surveyor's only daughter, Helena Jane Wesolowski, was born in 1845, at Pine and Market Street (church property presently). Village of Mount Clemens, lot 9, section ten, as in liber M, page 230. Education required, she was still in school after her 16th birthday, a rarity in the 1860's. The 5′5″ auburn-haired, hazel-eyed beauty was married at the age of 22 on Wednesday, July 10, 1867, to William H. McGarvey, a merchant from Petrolia, Ontario, in Mount Clemens by Reverend H. E. Bissell. The Polish reception was held at Ludwik's 5.6 acre estate on North Avenue at Market Street (church property presently). Helena became the first Michigan multi-millionairess from oil operations in Canada, Austria, Galicia, and the world's largest oil refineries in Trieste. She died in December 1897 in her mammoth castle, overlooking the canal locks at Port Gorlice, Galicia.

Speaking six languages, Ludwik Wesolowski, the retired surveyor, only enjoyed his daughter's early wealth, as he died on November 20, 1870, at New Baltimore, Michigan, always proud of his Polish heritage. He is buried in the Mount Clemens Clinton Grove Cemetery, and since 1915, Section A, lot 234, has been maintained without a visit from a relative, friend, or voter. Nor did he expect at death that his vivacious glamorous granddaughter would become Countess Mamie Helena Graf von Zeppelin, at the most festive of the century's three day wedding in Vienna, commencing on Thursday, November 12, 1896, alongside the banks of the green "waltzing" Blue Danube canal.

Today, with a name like Wesolowski, Ludwik would enjoy the Polish festivities throughout all of Michigan, were 4½ million residents have Slavic blood. Their ancestors, witnessing the 1853 European "war cloud" and the Crimean War of 1854, came to the middle west as foresters for the vast Michigan lumbering operations and the Studebaker mill in Indiana.

8
THE FIRST ELECTED SLAVIC POLITICIAN IN THE U. S.

An advertisement in the Thursday, July 27, 1844, issue of the Mount Clemens (Michigan) Patriot stated "L. Wesolowski, Deputy County Surveyor, 'Civil Engineering, Mapping, Drawing, and Land Surveying' " (Burton Historical Library Archives).

Ludwik Wesolowski was an assistant engineer on the Huron-Kalamazoo Canal Project. When the project failed financially, he obtained the deputy county surveyor's position, due to his outstanding education in Warsaw's University (Poland) of Military Engineering (Polish Library, 6 *d quai d'Orleans*, 75004 Paris).

Since he planned to remain in America, on April 11, 1846, he took his oath of naturalization at Mount Clemens, Michigan (recorded in Liber A, page 26 and 27, Macomb County Records).

He did swear to support the Constitution, and "that I do absolutely renounce and abjure forever all allegiance and fidelity to any foreign prince, potentate, state and sovereignty whatever, and particularly do absolutely and entirely renounce and adjure all allegiance and fidelity to 'Nicholas, the first Emperor of Russia and King of Poland, whereof I was heretofore a subject.' "

Renouncing the Emperor of Russia must have been pleasing to Ludwik, as he had fought the Russians in the Insurrection of November 29, 1830, while a student in Warsaw. Subsequently, he was detained by the Kingdom of Austria, then deported from Trieste by Chancellor Metternich on November 22, 1833. He arrived in New York on the night of March 28, 1834, and the following day he was given 33 dollars by the Austrian Consul Baron Lederer and, in essence, told "you're on your own" (Polish Library, Paris). Ludwik must have said to himself the old Polish proverb, "*Poki swiat swiatem, nie bedzie Niemiec Polakow bratem,*" which translated means "World without end, the German (Austrian) to the Pole will not be a friend."

In the summer of 1834, Wesolowski was in the Detroit to Port Huron area scouting for farm and forest land that Congress promised to grant the "Novembrists," as repayment for the services of the Polish soldiers, Pulaski and Kosciusko, for their heroic roles during the Revolutionary War. On September 9, 1834, at Detroit, the Polish scouting group wrote to their "benefactors" in New York City that the land was occupied and they were returning east, or might travel west. One member of this group, John Rychlinski, became a prominent engineer in St. Louis, Missouri (Archives, Polish Museum, Chicago, Illinois).

Wesolowski, speaking six languages, remained in Detroit and subsequently obtained a draftsman job on the proposed Canal project.

In the 1846 election, Ludwik received two write-in votes for County Surveyor, under the Whig Party. He resided in Clinton Township with his wife Sarah Jane (nee Fletcher), son Albert Z., age 8, and daughter Helena Jane, age 3. A son Charles was born on March 3, 1849 (tombstone, Petrolia, Ontario, cemetery).

The election of November 5, 1850, records reveal that Wesolowski was elected County surveyor, receiving 1161 votes of the 2160 votes cast, under the Whig Party.

Ludwik lost in 1852 to a George E. Adair, a Democrat, receiving 1253 votes to Adair's 1446 votes, due to the third party candidate, Austin Burt, who received 467 votes under the American Party candidacy, as Michigan's politics were in turmoil.

In the November 4, 1856, election, Ludwik received 1988 votes out of the 4080 votes cast; hence, losing again by under 200 votes in Macomb County.

The November 4, 1862, election records show that Wesolowski ran as a Democrat for the County Surveyor and won by receiving 1923 of the 3811 votes cast. This was an upset, as a Republican was in the White House, and the Civil War was in progress, but the Republican lost in Macomb County. Ludwik witnessed his son Albert enlisting in the Union Army at Mount Clemens in 1862 with Company F, 22nd Michigan Infantry.

With these election results, excellently documented in the Macomb County Clerk's Office, Wesolowski was the first person of Slavic extraction to become an elected official in the United States.

Today in Macomb County, Michigan, where over 65% of the electorate have Slavic blood in their veins, some dating back six generations in Michigan, Wesolowski would be overjoyed if he could be resurrected, as with his personality and surname no other person would dare run against him, especially under the Democratic Party. His slogan would be "WIN WITH WESOLOWSKI," or "WWW" for Senator.

OATH OF NATURALIZATION.—Bagg, Barns & Co., Printers, Booksellers and Bookbinders, Woodward Avenue, Detroit.

We Aaron Weeks & John J Leonard of Macomb County and State of Michigan, do swear that the petitioner, Ludwick Wesolowski has resided within the limits, and under the jurisdiction of the United States of America five years, and within the State of Michigan one year; that is to say, he, the said Ludwick Wesolowski resided in Clinton in the County of Macomb and State of Michigan

~~all which places are~~ within and under the Constitution of the United States;—and that during his residence within the United States, he has behaved as a man of good moral character, attached to the Constitution of the United States, and well disposed to the good order and happiness of the same,

A Weeks
John J Leonard

Sworn and Subscribed in open Court, this 11th day of April A D 1846
T. J Rutter Dept Clerk

I Ludwick Wesolowski do swear that I will support the Constitution of the United States, and that I do absolutely and entirely renounce and abjure forever all allegiance and fidelity to any foreign prince, potentate, state and sovereignty whatever, and particularly do absolutely and entirely renounce and abjure all allegiance and fidelity to Nicholas the first Emperor of Russia & King of Poland whereof I was heretofore a subject.

Ludwik Wesolowski

Sworn and Subscribed in open Court, this 11th day of April A D 1846
T. J Rutter Dept Clerk

OATH OF ENGINEER FROM DISMEMBERED POLAND

Wesolowski was a draftsman, engineer, and elected to the important position of County Surveyor in 1850 under the Whig Party.

Nicholas I, Emperor of Russia, was never considered King of Poland by the Poles, whose country was dismembered by Austria, Prussia, and Russia.

Notice that *Ludwik* is in his signature, indicating his dignity at the time of naturalization, dated April 11, 1846.

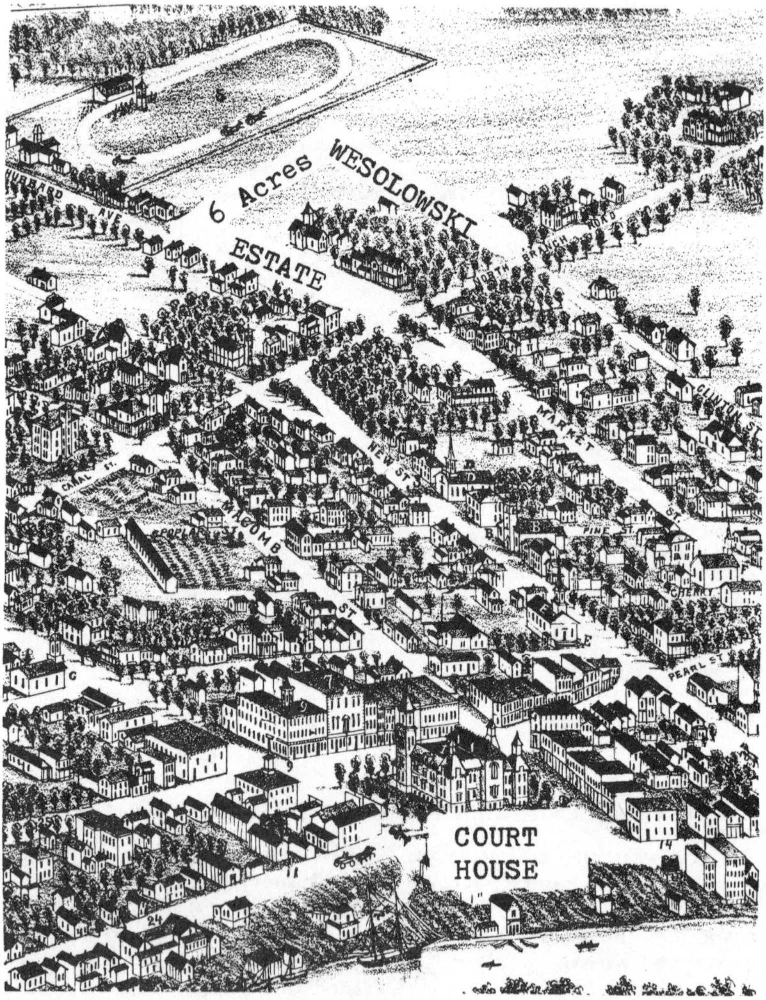

A POLISH AMERICAN ESTATE IN 1851

Ludwik Wesolowski built the colossal home, huge barn and smokehouse after being elected County Surveyor in 1850. Note the large orchard. Daughter Helena Jane was born in the home on the NW corner of Pine and Market Street, Village of Mount Clemens in 1845. Copy obtained through the courtesy of the Mount Clemens Library staff.

9
FINANCING A POLISH HOME

In the records of the Register of Deeds Office which are very accurate and a pleasure to work with, the Macomb County, Michigan, records in liber N, page 162, reveal that a Pole obtained a loan for the balance of his house payment.

Ludwik Wesolowski, the Macomb County Surveyor, on August 11, 1851, obtained a loan of $100 for the balance of the purchase price of said premises. The premises were located on the then North Branch Road, which today is on North Avenue at Market Street in the City of Mt. Clemens, Michigan.

The loan was obtained from an Arthur J. Robertson of Inverness, Scotland. The total amount of the repayment of the loan was in the amount of $131.25, payments per year were $43.75.

The Macomb County records reveal that the loan was paid in full on October 11, 1855.

It should be noted that money for mortgages in that time of history were obtained from Europe. Wealthy Europeans had agents in Michigan comparable to financial institutions and persons today when obtaining a mortgage or land contract.

Wesolowski built a beautiful home on 5.6 acres on the North Branch Road, and such acreage included an orchard, and from prints the orchard had over fifty trees.

Across the North Branch Road between the present Market Street and Clinton Street, Wesolowski also owned that land where he maintained another orchard.

To the west of Wesolowski's home were huge vegetable gardens. Further west of Wesolowski's home was a sulky race track.

It should be noted that this was the third home for Wesolowski and it could be stated that when he came to Michigan in 1834 he settled in Macomb County as a surveyor.

From all the records gleaned, this is considered the first loan in the State of Michigan by a person of Polish extraction in order to pay the balance of the purchase price for his third and huge home which had in excess of twelve rooms.

10
FIRST ORDAINED POLISH PRIEST--U. S.

"Obliging to advise that the Provincial Archives of Ma-*lopolskiej* are very scanty regarding information of Father Kasper Matoga, S.J.," said the *Kustosz Archiwum* (Arhivist). He then said that Kasper Matoga was born on December 30, 1823, birthplace being *Siepraw*, near *Myslenic*, the district of *Bochnia*, therefore, being a Pole. This village is 42 miles directly south from downtown cultural Krakow.

Matoga entered the Jesuit Order on August 11, 1845, at *Stary Wsi*, near *Brzozowa*. He was a novice for two years, 1845 to 1847, and a colleague of Francis Xavier Schulak (*The Sailing Missionary* by Natsolim, an unpublished book about Father Schulak, S.J.). The school year of 1847-48, these students studied at *Starej Swi*, where humanities (liberal arts) and rhetoric were the main subjects of their education.

"The exact date of Matoga's departure from Poland, unfortunately we cannot give," advised the Archivist.

In 1848 at Galicia, there was a persecution against the Polish priests, especially the Society of Jesus.

However interesting, although not always reliable, Spetz in his history of the Catholic Church in the County of Waterloo, Ontario, Canada, at page 254, says, "during the summer of 1848, Matoga walked from *Stare Wris* to Paris, France, where he became a member of the "*Missio Neo EBoracensis*," or the New York-Canadian Mission of the French Province.

The father superior of the French Province immediately sent Matoga to study for the priesthood at St. John's College (presently Fordham University). From 1848 to 1852, at Fordham University, Kasper studied philosophy and theology and was ordained in 1852 according to the Society of Jesus records, New York Province. Father Kasper Matoga, S.J., became the first priest of Polish extraction to be ordained in the United States and remain in the North American continent for the rest of his life.

After ordination, he travelled to Buffalo, New York, on his way to the opening of the Guelph, Ontario, newly established Jesuit Missionary Post. Father Matoga's first missionary assignments were in Northern Wellington, Bruce and Grey, making the scenic tours mostly on foot.

At the time, there were over 20,000 Catholics scattered throughout Western Canada and as "Far West as Lake Huron and the Georgian Bay" (*Les Jesuites du Canada*, Father Le Compte).

Travelling by canoe and sailing vessels, but mainly by foot, Father Matoga arrived in the Detroit area where he spoke to the French leaders. Besides the French language, Father Matoga spoke and wrote English, German, Latin, and Polish (Le Compte).

The Slavic people in 1853 attended Old St. Mary's Church in Detroit, Michigan (marriage records), but the church records were not scrutinized to determine if the "Soul Hunter" baptized any Germans or Poles.

Father Matoga went from Detroit to the Port Huron-Sarnia area, thence a vessel passage to the then beautiful virgin-timbered Georgian Bay, where the Irish and German Catholic immigrants farmed, fished, and forested.

Father Matoga immediately divided his apostolate into sectors from ten to twenty miles, varying according to the Catholic population. He would traverse this area five or six times per year, over trails which then were marked only by felled trees.

On the day of his appearance in each pastoral group, always scheduled in advance, the priest distributed the sacraments and taught catechism. Religious instruction (Bible) took place without respite from early morning and, after a sparse meal, he returned in the afternoon to pursue his apostolic rounds.

Only allowing himself a few days rest at the Jesuit residence at Guelph, he was termed "*INDEFESSUS ANIMARUM VENATOR*" (the indefatigable hunter of souls) by a visitor at the residence, in a letter to the Society General (Archives, *Les Fontaines, Chantilly, Republique Francaise*).

Possessing this physical and mental energy, Father Matoga's magnificant apostolate "aroused the fury of hell." The then powerful Orangists made attempts on his life, but "God turned away the bullets." They then "poured out vicious slander about this angelic young man" (Le Compte).

Mostly on foot on long tours, Matoga's troubles and excessively fatiguing duties afflicted him about thirty miles from Guelph with a throat disease (like diptheria). He walked home to Guelph, arriving speechless, and remained so till his death on August 21, 1856, at the age of 32. Others have stated that it was angina pectoris,

He lived a very full life in such a short span. Father Kasper Matoga, S.J., is buried at the Jesuit Mission Cemetery, Guelph, Ontario.

Fifty years later, in 1906, *The Sailing Missionary* (by NATSOLIM), Father Francis X. Schulak (Szulak, Shulak), a colleague at the noviate in 1845, where both took their first vows, travelled to Guelph where he offered a mass for his classmate, the "Indefatigable Hunter of Souls."

Father Schulak then came to Detroit where on August 1, 1906, the Detroit Jesuits gave him $54.00 travelling money on his way to Lourdes (Father Mataushek's letter to the *Malopolskiej* Provencial Superior). After the Lourdes pilgrimage Father Schulak returned to Krakow, where he died a few years later, after serving 63 years in the Order, over 50 years in missionary work (Archives, Society of Jesus, Roma, Italy).

It is almost a miracle that the two intellectual Slavic persons commenced their noviate together and labored in the Great Lakes area as missionaries. Father Matoga was the first person of Polish extraction ordained in the United States, only 76 years after the Declaration of Independence.

On your visit to Canada, visit the grave of Father Matoga. If you visit Krakow, Father Schulak is buried at the Jesuit Cemetery in *Maliepolska*. These uncanonized "Slavic Saints" will hear your prayers.

Only 42 miles due south of Krakow, visit the birthplace of the "Hunter of Souls," who was the first U.S. ordained Pole. Most of Polish Jesuit missionaries came from Galicia. At the Archives of the Province of *Malopolskiej* of the Society of Jesus, at *Maly Rynek* 8, Krakow, see the Keeper of the Archives, Alois Furczyk, S.J., for information about these two "saintly" missionaries. Clip this article and take it with you on your next visit to Poland because, if it wasn't for the cooperation of the scholarly Father Furczyk, this article could never have been written. *Wdzieczny Natsolim.*

11
POLES NEVER PERISH

For nearly five decades almost all of the history books were read regarding the Poles under Prussian oppression. The books, mostly history books, were scrutinized and were from all versions regarding the Germanization, or the attempted Germanization, of the Prussian-dominated Poles. But what is written here is from the historians of neutral nations, hence neither a Polish or a Prussian view.

The writer's ancestors left the forests and farmlands of Pomerania and Poznan, arriving in Michigan during the Civil War. Such ancestors purchased land in Michigan (National Archives), paying $14.00 for 160 acres. This virgin forest land was homesteaded.

This chapter and possibly the book was prompted years ago when it was read that the prussian Chancellor said, "Beat the Poles so that they lose the will to live. Personally I sympathize with their situation but we want to exist. There is thus nothing left to us but to exterminate them."

The Poles knew that eventually they would overthrow such genocidal tyrants (the Prussians), as the Poles have *ENDURANCE.*

The idea of the overthrow and return to independence started with the Polish intellectuals, students and artisans, not the wealthy bourgeoise. Polish self-education groups started when they commenced to perpetuate the Polish language and heritage.

Polish lands ruled by the Prussians would be similar to Ontario trying to rule Michigan, or in reverse, Michigan trying to rule Ontario's land.

It all began when the Crimean War was in progress. Other nations wanted Prussia on their side. When the "Paris Poles" no longer were the leaders of occupied Poland, the Poles realized that their destiny lied with the Poles in the provinces of Poznan and Pomerania.

This Polish independence even went to publication when in 1859 the newspaper *Poznan* Daily was first published. This newspaper's primary aim was to perpetuate the Polish heritage without the use of armed forces and violence.

The Poles knew that the Germans needed these provinces primarily for the farm products and the forests. Why the Prussians lacked foresight to see that they could never rule the Poles is attributable to Prussian leaders and unwillingness on the part of the Prussians to admit defeat and not realizing that the Pomeranian and Poznanian farmers and foresters knew that their ENDURANCE would overcome Prussian tyranny eventually.

Around 1850 the Poles owning land (farm and forest) had to mortgage such land due to the demand of the Prussians. The bad harvests of the three years, 1853 through 1855, resulted in foreclosures. With this financial tactic the Prussians acquired 300,000 acres of land, hence such 300,000 acres were lost by the original owners up to the year 1860.

Commencing in 1854 and up to 1870, most of the Poles that lost their farms and forest emigrated to the West, many settling in the Great Lakes area, where land was plentiful and the forest untouched.

After losing their farms and forests, Prussia expelled such Poles; Prussian police began the illegal search and seizure of all Polish homes; eliminating Polish in all public records; and no Polish language was allowed in the courts in these provinces.

The conflict between the Catholic Poles and the Protestant Germans also hit its peak in this era.

The Poles knew that eliminating the Polish language was a violation of the human law and a violation of the divine law, hence enhancing one of their great qualities, the quality of ENDURANCE.

To prompt the continuance of a Polish nation, a Polish language and a Polish culture, the newspapers then in publication said: "Polish first, Catholic after that."

The Prussians even removed the Polish coat-of-arms from all of the buildings, such buildings built by the Poles on Polish land. This is the proverbial 'insult to injury' that everyone uses.

In the city of *Chelmno*, which is in the province of Pomerania, a newspaper did what the *Poznan* Daily did, both declaring that people be allowed to speak and write in the Polish language.

The Prussian governor of the Poznan Province in 1863 made it impossible for any Pole to reside under Prussian tyranny, so more emigration followed in the year of 1863, many of such Poles coming to the Great Lakes area.

Also in 1863 the Poles celebrated the Christian millennium, and Archbishop Przyluski was in an advanced age and would retire. Upon his retirement a few years later Count Ledochowski was appointed Archbishop of Poznan. Whoever made this appointment can list this appointment as the mistake of the century, as Ledochowski could not even speak fluent Polish because the Count spent most of his time away from Poland.

Upon his orders, Ledochowski immediately said:

1. No political appearances by clergy.
2. Eliminating the Polish hymn "*Boze cos Polske*" in the Polish churches.
3. Priests cannot vote.
4. Closed a Polish Jesuit school.
5. Eliminated the priests from certain positions which priests had held for centuries.

Prussia in this period enacted a statute of migration, and Poles in droves left Prussian dominated Poland.

During the 1860's, Poznan had about two Polish Catholics to every German Protestant, and Jews only constituted about two per cent.

With the Poles, the Germans also kept on emigrating from these provinces, mostly to the New World, which was America, as even the Germans could not find compatibility with the Prussian rules.

During this time a railroad was constructed from Berlin to *Poznan* City and *Bydgoscz*, then to the town of *Wrzesnia*. From these areas the trains westward to Berlin were filled with Poles (and Germans, too). Then to Hamburg (sometimes Bremen) where they boarded vessels for passage to America, the land of the free.

The Prussians did not want the Poles to emigrate, as all the Poles worked the farms and forests and all of Europe needed food and lumber.

From 1861 to 1885 the Polish people either through foreclosure or departure for America lost, sold, or abandoned 750,000 acres of their land.

In all these problems encountered by the Prussians, the Poles were responsible for the irritation of the Prussians and such irritation started in order that the Poles protect their Polish culture.

The Prussian Chancellor should have known that he could never assimilate the Polish Catholics with the Protestant Germans. This combination cannot agree or assimilate in any other part of the world.

The Poles in Poznan and Pomerania were not docile as the Germans to (in) the west (meaning the Germans on German land). Such Poles had secret Polish schools in addition to the forced German schools, plus these Poles always read the Polish press. The Polish press at that time was considered to be humorous; however, the Prussians were never educated in Polish, hence the Prussians never realized the sincerity and eventual uprising of the Poles.

In the early 1870's the Prussians eliminated all Polish, even in teaching. Polish writing, as an elective, was not allowed.

The Archbishop could not stop the passive resistance. Eventually Ledochowski was imprisoned by the Prussians. After two years in prison, he retired to Rome.

For over twelve years there was no Archbishop of Poznan. It seems that when Poland was down as a nation, Poland had no friends. Why no archbishop was appointed for twelve years, this question alone would be a study if the archives would be open for a scholarly research.

The Poles continued to oppose the Prussians from all directions.

The Polish farmers and foresters demanded higher prices and they received such higher prices for their produce and products.

The farmers increased their acreage of potatoes and sugar beets, which were in great demand throughout Europe in that time of history. The Poles sold their lumber, timber, cattle, and grains, and by eliminating the German middle man they kept the money received in their villages for expansion in the purchase of more farm and forest lands.

In 1886 the Chancellor set aside 100 million marks to purchase land and forests from the Polish people, with the phrase, "Germans, but with German wives, not Polish one." This was reversed by the Poles who bought more land than they sold so the Prussian problems expanded.

The Poles recollected the Polish slogan which was in the Poznan Daily in 1865, saying then of the Prussian promises, "Let's not fool ourselves," so they continued with their endurance, and knew that the Prussians would perish. What a prophecy.

With this Polish endurance came solidarity of all the

Poles, peasant to prince, farmer, forester, and factory worker.

The Prussians constructed schools, universities, libraries, and theaters after 1900, but the Prussians had to construct such edifices as the Prussians then were in the minority and were "on the run."

What was lost, and Prussia realized too late, was that the emigrating Poles were the more robust and enterprising ones, and such Poles could not be replaced by importing Germans from Germand land. This forced emigration gave America the robust and enterprising Poles, many coming to the Great Lakes area.

Germanization never succeeded because 50% of the Polish homes became school rooms (school houses), where secretly Polish culture and heritage was taught. The Poles had secret signs, codes, and the vernacular. For over 150 years such secrets were handed down from generation to generation. All such secrets, codes, etc., was unlawful, but could a minor Prussian official penalize school boys, where most of the residents and school children were Poles?

The Poles had their own *ROLNIK* (farmer) groups in each community. This group sold to the Poles products and produce at an equitable price. The group really was a group to "Buy Polish and sell Polish" which the Prussians never did detect was the reason for the formation of these *ROLNIK* groups.

The Prussians in all of their ruthless years against the Poles could never win the confidence of the Poles.

How could the Prussians expect to assimilate the Poles, if they never could win the confidence of the Poles and never knew that the Poles are ENDURING?

This endurance factor has been with the Michigan Poles since before the Civil War. That is the reason Americans of Polish extraction are still proud of their Polish blood, culture and heritage.

12
WHY THEY CAME TO MICHIGAN

The Poles commenced immigrating to Michigan in 1854. They immigrated from the provinces of Pomerania and Poznan. The big groups came from the area of Bydgoscz, which is presently about 100 miles south of the port of Danzig. The Poles came to Michigan because they came from a region where there were immense lumbering and woodworking industries.

Not many of the Poles in the Great Lakes area have any knowledge of the land that their ancestors came from. This chapter is written to explain a little of what the Great Kingdom of Poland was in times past.

Poland was a vast plain with no natural frontiers. The Vistula River flowed through the center of Poland. From the north to the south, Poland was about 713 miles; and from east to west, about 693 miles.

There was good pasture and arable land, and, of course, the northern part had many beautiful forests. In the eastern part of then Poland in certain parts there was sand and swamp.

Wheat, barley, rye, and other cereals were the crops primarily raised.

There were iron, copper, and lead mines and vast coal and salt mines.

In the fertile fields they had village communities.

The Latin language was used as the literary medium; hence, a person would have to have knowledge of the Latin language to study the early history of Poland.

It is alleged that the geographer Ptolemy in the Second Century A.D. named it Poland, implying that the dwellers were of the plains.

The downfall of the Great Kingdom of Poland came when the Saxon kings, who were from Saxony and who could not speak the Polish language, became the kings of the Great Kingdom of Poland; hence, the downfall of Poland.

Another downfall of Poland was the ever-increasing encroachment of the Prussian people. It is known that around the year 1200 the Poles in the Silesian territory had their own coin known as the Milost.

As many of the records of Poznan, Poland, indicate, some of the Poles who came to Michigan had the following last names: Magner, Mock, Mayer, Malos, Melka, Maap, Miast, Mathias, Miller, Mezger, Meyer, Nast, plus many others. The amazing thing is that the people with these surnames had Polish fathers, Polish mothers, and they were baptized in the church of Poznan in Poland in the year 1825.

13
FIRST POLISH FARMER IN MICHIGAN

The assimilated Michiganders, whose great-grandparents and, in some instances, great-great-grandparents were homesteading farmers, possibly do not realize that their ancestors were foresters and of Polish extraction. Hence, this article is written in tribute to these great persons who came to the Middle West. They had an education, a profession, and a "few" gold coins. They were not the peasants described by many writers of Slavic history. Such writers have no conception of what the Pomeranians, Poznanians, Kashubians, Danzingers, and Silesians did for this area as they established the trend of Slavic emigration.

In the spring of 1853, after completing his schooling and his 17th birthday, Martin Baranowski arrived in Detroit, as he was sent from Poznan (then German Poland) by his father "to keep him out of the Army." (Affidavit, National Archives). Speaking two languages, plus reading and writing Polish, Latin and German, the 5′6″ (about two inches taller than the then average height of 5′4″), dark-complexioned, grey-eyed, brown-haired affable youngster became a laborer, awaiting the rest of his family to arrive next year.

Martin's younger brother Joseph, before leaving Poland in March, 1854, said in his affidavit, "I was freed from school as at that time Germany had a compulsory school law compelling children to attend school between the ages of seven to fourteen years" (National Archives).

The end of March of 1854, Martin's entire family arrived in Detroit. His father, Forester Joseph Baranowski (the elder, as there is no Junior in Poland), with his wife, Rose (nee Gotseit), and their other nine children, were greeted by an economic depression.

Cholera was raging the country in July, 1854, and everybody was stricken. Rose, the mother, and son Frank died, and Forester Joseph barely recovered. He thought of returning to Poznan, in German-controlled Poland, but with the remaining nine children he thought of the "war clouds"; the Crimean War, and the other, as his "real reason he emigrated to America, to keep his boys out of the German Army." (National Archives Records) After the cholera, "the house was thoroughly fumigated" and "no doubt mother's books and records were then destroyed."

With this conscription in his mind, and because of the depression and the slow recovery from cholera in Detroit, Baranowski settled on a farm in Ottawa County, Michigan, in 1854.

Joseph Baranowski, born in 1805 in Poznan, Poland, became a farmer with a forestry background. In the census of July 11, 1860, of the Township of Wright, Post Office, Berlin (now Marne), Michigan, Ottawa County, on page 101, the census enumerator misspelled his name, Jos. Bernowski (one mistake), age 55, place of birth listed as Germany (second mistake). His real property was valued at $800.00 (upper middle class in pre-inflationary Civil War era of 1860), and personal property value was $100.00. He had two minor daughters in school, and a 16 year old son at home, plus a domestic, age 28.

Forester-Farmer Baranowski's son, Joseph, born March 17, 1840, in Poznan, Poland, was working in the Grand Rapids area as a farmer and laborer in 1861 when he consulted his father regarding the Civil War. The elder Joseph said, "I cannot prevent you from going, as you are of age." On September 4, 1861, he enlisted for the Civil

War, with Company F, Second Michigan Cavalry. (National Archives)

Baranowski re-enlisted on January 5, 1864, and was appointed bugler and paid $400.00 for the prior service. After a distinguished war record, he was honorably discharged on August 17, 1865, at Macon, Georgia, and his name was listed as Barnoski, Baranski, Bonaski, and Barnoshern (Civil War Records, NA). The company muster-out roll, dated August 17, 1865, reveals that he received $190.00, as he was charged $10.16 for one pair of pliers, one sabre belt, and one screw driver.

With the bounty money received, young Baranowski purchased a farm in the Township of Wright, R.F.D. Route One, Berlin, Ottawa County, Michigan. So in 1865, Joseph Baranowski was the second generation farming in Michigan, which would place him as the earliest farmer, the son of a Polish farmer.

The June 29, 1870, census of Wright Township, Ottawa County, Post Office, Berlin, on page 38, lists Joseph Bernoski, a farmer, real estate value of $1,000.00, personal property at $320.00, born in Poland. He was a U. S. citizen, and his wife was Helen (nee Hodges), born in New York. Son Edward, age two, and daughter Ella was born on February 12 of the census year.

The son of the first Polish farmer in Michigan died on March 22, 1924, 84 years and five days of age, of organic heart disease, a retired farmer having two wives and eleven children.

From 1853 to 1867 the foresters came to Michigan and Indiana and took advantage of the Homestead Acts, especially the Subsequent Act of 1862, as they were rugged, educated, independent in mind, hard workers, and not afraid to be "nomadic."

These foresters settled in Branch County, Wayne County, and other Michigan areas, and in Noble and St. Joseph

County, Indiana, where they were employed by the Studebaker Company. Subsequently they ventured as foresters into Alpena and Presque Isle County, Michigan, and obtained 160 acres of land for $14.00 or about nine cents per acre. At this price, the Poles were not dumb in buying the land. Yes, there have been Polish farmers in Michigan since 1854, so the Poles have toiled the Michigan soil for over a dozen decades.

14
ASPARAGUS POLONAISE

When the foresters from the provinces of Pomerania, Poznan and Gdansk arrived in Branch and St. Joseph Counties, Michigan, prior to the Civil War, these Poles were amazed at the beautiful asparagus growing in Michigan.

In their employment as foresters and in the lumbering businesses, these Poles noticed that the asparagus was growing alongside of the footing of the railroad bed. They also realized that the asparagus was similar to the asparagus that was grown in Poland and also the asparagus that was grown alongside of the beautiful highways in Poland.

These foresters immediately informed their wives and relatives, who purchased some Michigan plants and transplanted the wild asparagus roots in their huge gardens. The Polish women also planted asparagus seed knowing that such plants would require three years to reach maturity and to produce asparagus that was to be consumed.

Having a balanced diet in that area of Poland was always a prerequisite in these provinces.

According to tradition, the asparagus would first appear in Poland on St. Stanislaus Day (May 8) and on that first day the *Szparag* Stanislaw would be served even in a small quantity. Every member of the family would get a taste of this spring delicacy; however, it was served primarily to the elders as asparagus was a spring remedy for senior citizens in Poland.

The writer's paternal (distaff) great grandmother handed down this universal recipe that originated in Poland. The recipe is:

Two bunches of tender asparagus

Three tablespoons of bread crumbs

Six ounces of unsalted butter

Four hard boiled egg yolks, chopped. (Duck eggs can be used).

Parsley, if available.

Cook the asparagus with the tender tips upwards in rapidly boiling water (add three pinches of salt if preferred–as the three pinches was a superstition of the Trinity).

Boil and steam the asparagus until tender.

Put asparagus in a hot serving dish or a hot metal holder.

Sprinkle with the bread crumbs that were fried in butter. Top with the finely chopped egg yolks and apply parsley if available.

What knowledge these Poles had over 150 years ago by serving this nutritious delicacy, as today it is known that senior citizens should consume green vegetables to retain proper nutrients.

Having bread, butter, eggs, and hot asparagus, this food preparation can be eaten at any meal.

15
POLISH CHAIN-MAN

Every research historian investigates the documentation of all writings of his place of birth and tries to obtain all of the facts regarding the infancy of his "hometown."

The first census of Alpena County, Michigan, was taken in the year of 1860. It commenced on June 1, 1860, by the then Assistant United States Marshall Walter L. Kellogg (National Archives). He commenced in the town of Fremont and then he started to enumerate the Village of Alpena. Both were in the same area, as Fremont became a part of Alpena, due to another Fremont in Michigan.

That year in the Village of Alpena there lived fishermen by the name of Carter and Lambert. Alpena had the Post Office, which included the Town of Fremont.

The census record lists on page 8, dated the 7th day of June, 1860, line 14, a person by the name of David D. Oliver. This is the same David D. Oliver who wrote the book "The Centennial History of Alpena County" which was published in 1903.

The 1860 census reveals that he was a lumberman in the town of Fremont and he had a value of real estate of $8,000.00 and a value of personal estate of $3,000.00. It gave his birthplace as New York. On the same page, in the residence building next door to this David Oliver was a boarding house where all the day laborers resided. Such laborers had no personal and real property, according to the census report, which in essence means that they did not have in total net worth the amount of $50.00. These laborers undoubtedly were employed by David Oliver, as in that era there were no commuters.

It is interesting to discover that on Line 25 of the same page of the census report there is an entry of A.S.A. MICHALOWSKY, who was listed as being 21 years of age, a day laborer, and his place of birth was Poland, and Michalowsky could read and write. This census documentation automatically gives Michalowsky the title of being the first resident Pole in that area of Michigan, when the northeastern region commenced development and settlement.

The initial A. and initial S. before Michalowsky's name is the abbreviation for the Anglo-Saxon, as undoubtedly the census enumerator encountered his first Slavic person and might have had difficulties with the name. Michalowsky, being employed by David D. Oliver and living next door to Oliver in the Village of Fremont, must have been an industrious person and a valuable man, as Micholowsky is mentioned in the book that was written by David D. Oliver.

Oliver reminisces in his writing concerning a road that has to be built from the AuSable River to Alpena, Michigan. Oliver stated that he made a contract to survey the road for the sum of $5.00 per mile "payable in county orders, or lands, at the option of the surveyors." The County Commissioner, of course, in April 1862 when the contract was made to survey the road, stated it would be "under his supervision"; however, Oliver would furnish all the things that were needed to accomplish this important survey in order to build a road from the area of the AuSable River to Alpena, Michigan. This road is part of the present US-23 Highway, and the roads east of US-23.

Oliver continued in his article that on May 31, 1862, he commenced the survey of the road at the AuSable River. He stated that his party consisted of a commissioner and a Daniel Carter and himself and they were looking out for the most feasible route for the road. It is also mentioned that one of the chain men was an A. J. A. Micholowsky. The chain man at that time of history had a good knowledge of mathematics, because there was such terminology as chains, links and, of course, furlongs in measurements. On the trip were two people named King and Isaacson who were the packers. Packers provided the transportation, either by horses, mules or oxen, and provisions for the complete survey crew. There was also a person by the name of Newell who was the axman and a Degroat who was the cook on the trip.

It must have been a very challenging and interesting job beginning that summer because in 1862 that region was all beautiful virgin forests. Mr. Oliver stated that in due time the survey was completed within the allocated time and a "report was accepted in Lansing in the fall of 1862." He further stated that in 1863 the first contracts were made for the work on the road.

Travelling by foot through the virgin forests, Michalowski and the survey group must have seen the beauty of the soaring eagles, the hawks, the cub bears, and the beaver, in addition to consuming the wild berries and other wild growing fruits that were prevalent at that time. As the newly laid-out road was always near water, there always was an abundant supply of numerous varieties of fresh fish. The writer vividly recollects when a youngster he would go to the fishing docks in Alpena to purchase fresh lake trout, whitefish, and in the spring of the year the lake herring, which would be marinated; and the remainder of the herring would be placed in the smoke house and when almost completely smoked the youthful eyes would be in tears from the smoke house door opening in order to taste test the delicacy. Smoked lake trout was the favorite.

It would be only conjecture on the part of the writer to state how Michalowski arrived in Alpena County. This will be left for some other historian or native of Alpena County, especially a person having Polish blood in his veins, who could write about him for posterity.

Michalowski must have been a very enduring person and not afraid of the exploration of the virgin forest. Being accepted for the crew, he had knowledge by that time of the English language, as the census report indicates, even though being only 22 years of age and born in Poland. Michalowski must have thought when he ventured from the AuSable River, beginning the journey into the dense virgin forest, of the Polish Proverb: "*Im dalej w las, tem gesciej drzew*," which in essence is that you should not be fearful in life and the translation would mean: the farther into the woods, the thicker the trees. It is obvious that life continues as it did in 1862 when Michalowski was the first Pole who was on a survey crew through the beautiful virgin forest of northeastern Michigan, in order that the first road be constructed.

When the planned divided highway is completed, that portion of highway US-23 could be called the A. J. A. MICHALOWSKI LAKESHORE THOROUGHFARE, the gateway to the majestic transcendent northeastern Michigan, adjoining the radiant azurean water of Lake Huron. With a sign with all those words, parents could test their children's reading ability, as they drove in that part of Michigan.

16
POLISH *PODPINKI*

Recorded history states that in the northern provinces of Poland the people were tall and lean due to the abundant foods that prevailed.

One of the Polish delicacies is what the Poles call a *grzyb* (mushroom); however, in the northern provinces of Poland they were given the word *podpinki*, which in essence is the same–a mushroom. These types of mushrooms were the young button type and are very succulent. When picking, the larger ones were used; however, only the caps were used.

Many of the stories of mushrooms were brought to the Middle West and the Great Lakes area by the Polish foresters, many of them becoming homesteading farmers. In Poland it was alleged that after the first frost in September these succulent button-type mushrooms would appear.

It was further said that the frost would appear after the first Friday after the *Matki Boskiej Zielnej* (Blessed Mother Feast of Greenery). On that day the harvest crops and produce would be taken to the church to be blessed.

This day usually preceded the Ember Days which were after September 14. It should be noted that the Ember Days at that time of history were days of fast and abstinence where no meat or meat derivative could be consumed.

This would be perfect timing as the people of the northern provinces of Poland would pick these mushrooms and the Saturday Ember Day main meal would be sauteed-in--butter mushrooms and fried-in-butter fresh fish.

It is known that mushrooms lack calories and it is this food and perch which is a perfect diet. Working in the forest, the addition of butter had no effect on these tall and lean natives of such provinces.

The forests of Poland were thinned for faster growth, and it is known that reforestation was practiced by the Poles since time immemorial.

The year following such thinning, after the first frost as stated above, a button-type mushroom was gathered during the village group mushrooming.

When the foresters from Poland arrived to work in southwestern Michigan during the 1850's and 1860's, there were many food gathering mushrooming parties.

These Poles then homesteaded, farmed, and obtained employment in northeastern Michigan, which was experiencing the beginning of the big lumber boom in 1870.

The Poles would pick these mushrooms, which reminded them of the mushrooms obtained in the peaceful forests of the northern provinces of Poland. After being picked, the mushrooms would be washed and rinsed at least six times. The young button-types which were very succulent were boiled. Only the caps of the large mushrooms were used. These caps were sliced and then threaded on a string and then dried in the sun—otherwise dried near the windows facing the south.

Later on, many of the mushrooms were canned in jars ranging up to two quarts in size, in addition to the mushrooms that were dried.

As each batch of mushrooms were boiled, an onion and a silver dime were placed in the huge kettle. It was a superstition that if the onion or dime turned black then the mushrooms were poisonous and had to be discarded.

The writer vividly recalls picking such *podpinki* mushrooms along the Wessel Road in Alpena, Michigan. After a quarry company cut down the timber, the following year produced the most abundant crop that was ever witnessed by the older generation in the history of northeastern Michigan. Such senior citizens claim they were the "tastiest," also.

The writer also recollects washing and rinsing the button mushrooms and cutting the stems from the larger ones, saving only the caps.

Reflecting back to the younger years, it is now deduced that the reason the silver dime was placed in the huge kettle was to get all of the younger members in the group to help in the washing, rinsing, boiling, and eventual canning of the mushrooms. When the task was completed, the kettle had to be scoured and cleaned, and whoever cleaned the kettle would be rewarded with a dime.

The ingenuity of the parents in placing a dime in the kettle was plain common sense, as it would be impossible to obtain ten pounds of mushrooms for a dime.

When the Poles continued to come to the Great Lakes area, they could be in the forest before daybreak usually in the month of September.

It was once rumored that there were certain spacemen walking in the forest after the first heavy frost in Michigan; however, by deduction, one can only state that it was more than likely a Polish person in a black fur coat with a flashlight picking the succulent young button mushrooms.

17
SOLVING THE CENSUS MISTAKES

It is well known that the Census of 1850 listed a Pole who immigrated to this country as being born in Poland. In the 1860 Census, from reviewing many census reports and passenger lists of ships, a person listed as being born in Poland in the 1850 Census was listed in the 1860 Census as being born in Prussia. This was possibly done by the census enumerator as no Poland existed due to the partition of Poland by Austria, Prussia, and Russia.

Many Polish historians and scholars all know that the census reports starting in 1860 never gave credit to the people of their Polish parentage due to Poland being confiscated.

The Census of 1880 in Posen Township, Presque Isle County, is an example of this. The writer is well acquainted with this township and county. The census, made by the attorney trained enumerator, reveals that 40% of the Poles residing in Posen Township are listed as being born in Prussia even though most of the remaining 60% of the Poles came from the same region but are listed as being born in Poland.

To solve the problem of actually how many Polish people there are in the United States would require a few months' work, if not longer, of checking the ship passenger lists.

The writer suggests that the Archives of the Hamburg passenger lists, from where most of the people came when immigrating to America, some of which are on microfilm in this country, be scrutinized to determine if these people actually came from Poland. It is a known fact that the Hamburg American Line sailing from Hamburg, Germany, has a passenger list starting from the year 1837 to the present time.

When larger ships were built, many of the Polish persons left from the port of Bremen. The North German Lloyd Line commenced sailing in 1856 from the port of Bremen.

The passenger lists of the ships from Hamburg list the persons that embarked from the port of Hamburg. It gives the date of embarkation, the husband's full name, the place of origin, the occupation, and the age; also the given names and the names of the wife and children and at times the port of destination. These Archives in Hamburg have an index and they are all at the Hamburg State Archives in Hamburg, Germany.

The passenger lists from Bremen, Germany, are in the Archives in Bremen. These Archives list all the passengers but the individual names are not indexed. Such index files were destroyed during World War II.

It is the contention of the writer that the passenger lists of both Bremen and Hamburg should be studied to determine how many people of Polish extraction came to this country because Austria and Prussia wanted the Poles to leave their land so the Austrians and Prussians could occupy the land that was owned by the Poles. In fact, Bismarck increased the compulsory military service to four years so the Poles would leave their land.

It is recommended that the Hamburg Archive records be checked from the year 1846 to the year 1882. The Archive records in Bremen, Germany, should be checked from the year 1856 to the year 1882. These records could then be computerized and projected.

All of the census reports of the United States, as above

stated, never gave credit to the people of Polish extraction. This task would require some student(s) to first check the records that are available in the United States and then, if incomplete, spend some time in Hamburg and Bremen, Germany.

Such researcher(s) should have the knowledge of the German language, a readable knowledge of the Latin language, and, of course, the knowledge of the Polish language.

This task would not be very difficult because, in addition to the surnames, the researcher(s) could check the first names. The first names of Polish people at that time are easily distinguished because there are names as Balbina, Jadwiga, Tekla, and then there are also Teofil, Stanislaw, Boleslaw, Bronislawa, Maciej, then of course the very common name of Casimir. Further Polish names were Josephine, Agneska, Wladyslawa, Pelagia, Anastasia, Sophie, Justina, Isador, Kasper, Antonina, in addition to such names of Jacob and Michalina. Then there was also Stefan, Aniela, and other Polish names.

If the researcher(s) had knowledge of Polish when checking these records, he could easily detect a Polish first name, or a Polish surname, and place of origin.

The Polish people for years have been writing articles regarding the census which never gave them credit as place of birth of Poland, due to Poland being invaded and partitioned by Austria, Prussia, and Russia.

In order to eliminate this continuous debate of the question, this question will not be solved until somebody undertakes the problem of going and checking the passenger lists in Hamburg and Bremen. It is from these two ports that most of the Polish people departed—their destination either being New York, Quebec, Boston, Philadelphia, Baltimore, and, of course, Charleston, in the southern state of South Carolina.

Unless this research is done and substantiated by projection, the Poles will continue the perennial argument: "We never received credit."

18
POLISH "PEANUTS"

The sunflower seed in Polish is called *slonecznik*. As there were no peanuts in the northern provinces of Poland, for various festivities and as Americans munch peanuts today, in Poland the children had their own version of Polish "peanuts." These "peanuts" in essence were the seed of the sunflower.

The sunflowers that were grown by the Poles in the area of Coldwater, Michigan, during the time of the Civil War were the type that had short stalks. The seeds were plump, meat filled, and had a thin shell.

A modified version of the roasted sunflower seeds was first used by the Poles during the Civil War. Subsequently this recipe was used by the Polish homesteaders in northeastern Michigan.

The recipe is:

Two tablespoons of sour salt (coarse salt) to each quart of water.

Two cups of sunflower seeds.

Bring to a boil, then lower the heat to a simmer for approximately an hour varying with the variety of the sunflower seed.

Drain the seeds well and place on paper towel to dry.

Then place the seeds on a buttered pan.

Bake in over at 225 degrees, stirring every fifteen minutes for an hour.

Sprinkle with salt as desired.

The grandparents and relatives on their huge 320 acre

farms must have been overly patient when they prepared the Polish "peanuts" for their sassy city-born and city-raised grandchildren when they invaded the farms.

The writer can vividly recollect feeding grandpa's trained talking crow, named *KRUK*, such Polish "peanuts."

But the eye glance reprimand was received from the good-natured grandfather, when the trained-in-Polish language crow began screaming "*psia krew*" (dog's blood), when the insistent grandchildren could not get *KRUK* to say Polish "peanuts" in English.

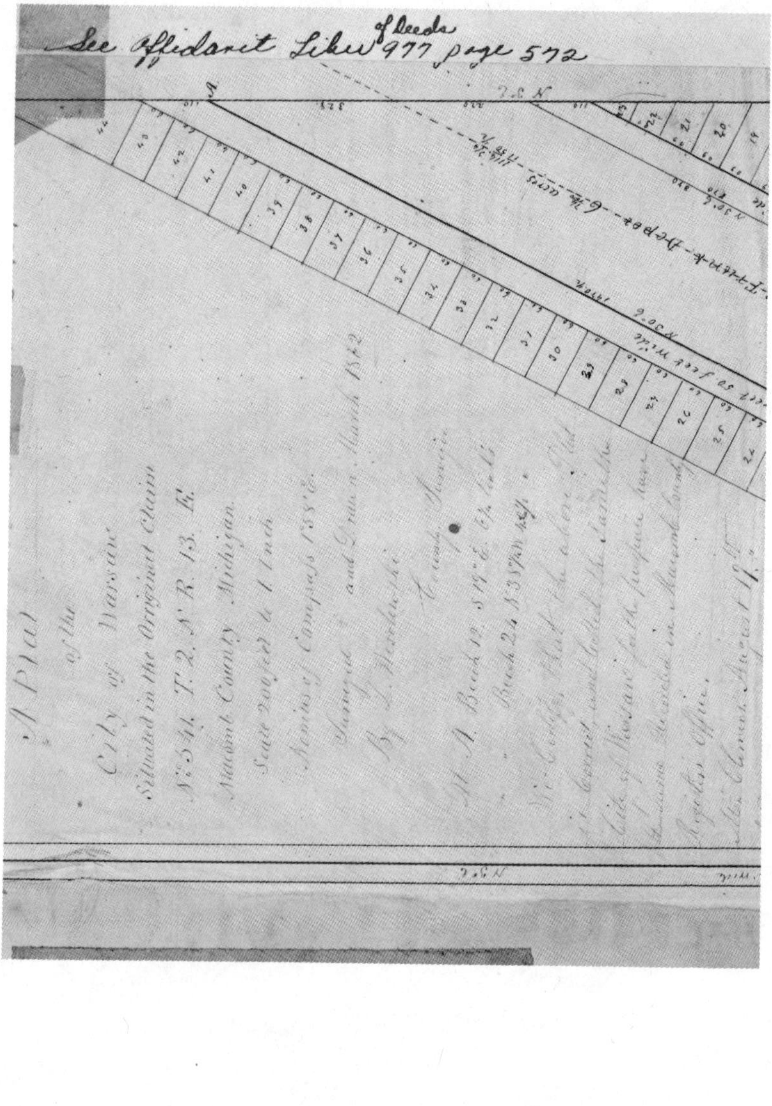
See Affidavit Liber of Deeds 977 page 572

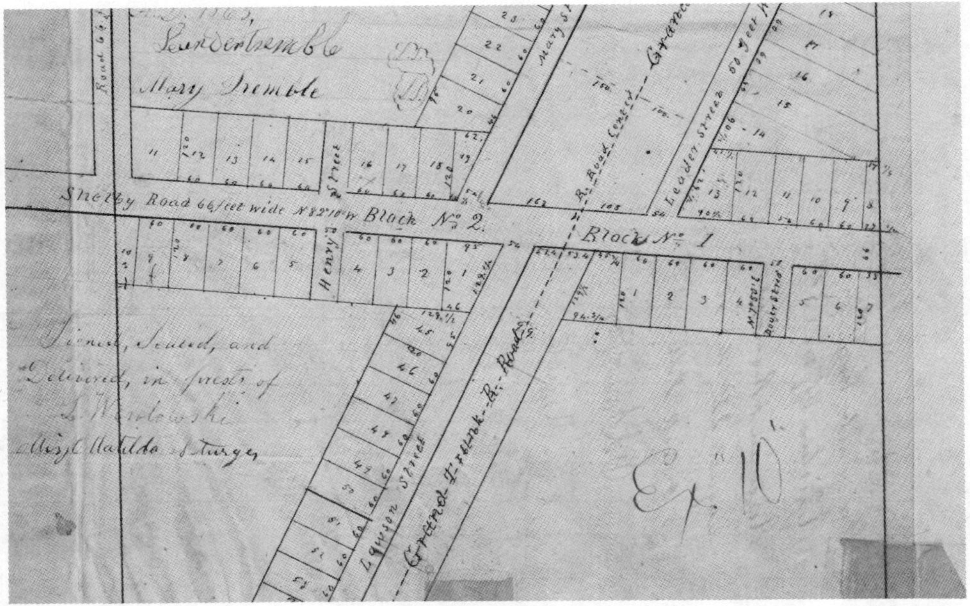

WARSAW, MICHIGAN–1862

A plat of the City of Warsaw, Michigan, was surveyed and drawn in March, 1862, by Ludwik Wesolowski, County Surveyor. Elected under the Democratic ticket, Wesolowski was victorious over the Republican. Very unusual during the Civil War Period, as President Lincoln was in the White House.

GRAND TRUNK R.R.
DEPOT
THOMAS A. EDISON WAS
EMPLOYED AT THIS R.R. DEPOT
IN WARSAW, MICHIGAN, WHICH
WAS SURVEYED, MARCH, 1862

19
CITY OF WARSAW, MICHIGAN

Elected as the County Surveyor in Macomb County in 1850 as the Whig Party candidate, and under the Democratic Party Platform during the Civil War, Ludwik Wesolowski, during March 1862, had surveyed and "drawn" the plat of the City of Warsaw, as recorded in Liber 47, page 621 and 621 A, Macomb County Records. The original paper, writing, etc., is intact and complete in the Register of Deeds Office, since 1865.

Situated presently in Mount Clemens, at Cass Avenue and the railroad tracks, the Warsaw plat included:

A. Block number one, east of the railroad tracks, consisted of 23 lots, having 60 foot frontages, and depth of 120 to 240 feet.

B. Block number two, west of the tracks, had 54 lots, with 60 foot frontage, and 120 feet in depth.

The streets in the plat were Shelby Road, Henry Street, Lawson Street, Dover Street; and Mary and Leander Street, named after the owners of the homestead property, Leander and Mary Tremble.

The Grand Trunk Depot area was on the north side of present Cass Avenue, being 270 feet in width along the old Shelby Road, according to the survey. The original passenger depot built during the summer of 1862, was east of the railroad track, and the warehouse was west of the track.

The nonious of the compass was one degree, 58 minutes east, in March 1862 in the explanation of the plat. This compass variation was explained many times to a youngster employed on the train named Edison, by the well educated Wesolowski.

On August 19, 1865, Leander and Mary Tremble certified that "the above plat is correct and called the same, the City of Warsaw for the purpose have the same recorded in Macomb County Registers Office." It was signed, sealed, and delivered in 'presents' of L. Wesolowski and a Matilda Sturgen.

The same day, L. Wesolowski, the first Notary Public of Polish extraction in Michigan, who could speak six languages, notarized the affidavit, saying in part, "Before me, a Notary Public, in and for said County, personally came . . . known to me the persons," who executed the foregoing . . . acknowledged . . . , and said Mary Trombley, on an examination separate and apart from her said husband, acknowledged that She executed the same freely and without the fear of anyone." This statement by the wife was adopted in Michigan during statehood, as Michigan has always treated women equally–long before any liberation movement.

Wesolowski's terminology as to the land and affidavit was comparable to that of the leading attorneys of that period in Michigan history. His handwriting was excellent, and the drawing of the plat to perfection, due to his earlier training at the university in Warsaw, Poland.

The Plat was received and recorded on August 22, 1865, at 5 o'clock p.m., and the original drawing is in the liber, intact and complete.

Warsaw was so named because Wesolowski, always a patriot for a cause, was born in Warsaw, Poland, on March 3, 1810. Driven out by the Confiscating Czarist rule in 1831, he was imprisoned by the Emperor of Austria, then deported by Chancellor Metternich, arriving in New York on March 28, 1834.

After the insurrection of 1863 in Poland, he listened to

the Polish immigrants about their last "chance in partitioned Poland," when he railroaded to his visits in Detroit, where the newly arrived Poles in Detroit, whose sons, the same as his Mount Clemens born (year 1842) son, Albert Z., enlisted in the Army for the Civil War; hence, certifying the Warsaw name in 1865, as then he knew he could never visit his relatives and friends in his homeland, even in old age.

It is said that Wesolowski built the largest smokehouse in the Warsaw, Michigan, area, in order to smoke his kielbasa, bacon, hams and *sledzie* (herring).

Educated in military engineering, Wesolowski knew after the Huron-Kalamazoo Canal financial failure that the railroad was the future of transportation in Michigan, and placing the City of Warsaw around the depot, transportation was very important for the development of any new area.

Over a century ago the logistical genius Ludwik Wesolowski was trying to explain and relay that railroads will never phase out in Michigan, and his prediction is applicable today, especially with the new plans of rapid transit.

Wesolowski is buried in the Clinton Grove Cemetery, on the old Shelby Road (Cass Avenue today), Mount Clemens. He is buried in a position so that, if Ludwik could raise his eyelids, he would be able to see the trains rolling along the merged old City of Warsaw and smile, as his prediction is a reality and a necessity in an energy crisis coupled with transportation problems.

20
POMERANIA PALATINE'S PRINCE *PIESEK*

Palatinate in Polish is termed *WOJEWODYTWA*, which is a district or territory, similar to a state in our Union, or a Province in Canada.

Professor Bobrzynski in his writing, *DZIEJE POLSKI w ZARYSIE*, In Volume Two, published in 1881 at Warsaw, Poland, explains the territories of such palatinates. In his Great Poland division, he lists some of the following divisions (territories), as:

A. *Poznan*.

B. Inowroclaw, where the present City of *Bydgosz* is situated.

C. *Pomorska* [Pomerania], the Baltic Sea Coast and southward to *Poznan*.

From these territories, the Polish people in 1854 commenced emigrating to the Great Lakes area in masses. They spoke and read Polish and German. In addition to writing in these two languages, they wrote in Latin, such Latin in a Gothic German script.

These Polish Provinces had excellent pasture land, arable agricultural land, timber yielding forests, and peaceful meadows.

The Provinces had Poles and Kashubes, and the people had a dialect of their own. One historian recorded that their language had harmony and melody, similar to the murmur of an oak of three hundred years, and not the plaintive (melancholy) and feeble cry of a reed, swayed by every wind. Some of the natives had a fluctuating accent and more nasal sounds. They were perfect in diction and elocution in their speech.

Their homes were made of brick, stone, or wood, and many homes had a combination of such construction materials.

The peaceful Pomeranian Poles enjoyed self-transportation by horseback, which was even used by their lean and slim women.

The winter clothes consisted of lambskin and sheepskin, with the wool-on. The summer seasons brought the use of a close-fitting coarse cloth version of pants, shirts and dresses.

This area had a sort of a habit, called a *samodzialka* (homespun of wool), which sleeves were woven and it was all of one piece. This habit could be worn by either sex, and was in different shades of a rustic color, and in sizes for all ages.

For centuries many nations tried to invade this fertile land, but were always repelled.

These Pomeranians and Poznanians witnessed the first dismemberment by Prussia in 1772. The unscrupulous and incompetent Prussians began directing (attempted governing) the area. These Poles only received evasive and unfavorable answers from such Prussians.

At the Treaty of Paris in 1856, the Poles were not even considered, and these Poles knew that they must depart from their centuries owned beloved homeland, as they could not tolerate any more *Kanikula* (dog days).

On February 8, 1863, Prussia agreed to try to end the Polish Insurrection, so these Pomeranians knew that they would depart immediately to join other Poles in the Great Lakes Region, even though America was entangled in the War of Rebellion. They sold their beloved land and forests that remained after the confiscation by the Prussians.

With the brief background and history of these Provinces, a story handed down from the first generation to the sixth generation Poles in Michigan is appropriate and timely, as these Poles developed a dog that is considered the best pet and companion.

In this territory of Pomerania, for centuries, the residents had sheep which required sheep dogs. The sheep herders and sheep ranchers continually tried to perfect a perfect sheep dog, and small in size. How the original sheep dog arrived in that part of Poland has never been recorded, and the many versions explained would only lead to mythology.

The Pomeranian Poles would take the smallest dog from a litter, then barter with a neighbor who had the smallest sheep dog, and they then bred the smallest, thereby developing the three pound dog. This method is similar to thoroughbred horse owners in evaluating pedigrees, for size, conformity, etc.

The breeding of the smallest dogs for over centuries, produced a dog weighing only four kilograms (three pounds), but with many factors and features.

The tiny dog was *Pokojowy* (peaceful), but had boldness. Such dog could be disciplined, followed instructions with proficiency, and had the most intelligence of any breed of dogs.

This dog was not distracted and "minded" his own business, which trait even the Pomeranian people possess, and even though bold, the dog was not vicious.

This diminutive dog was lively in temper and conduct; very quick and obedient.

Pomeranian dogs developed a double coat for the changeable weather, and was very hardy. It had a firm grip, possessed sturdiness, and it lived in excess of 25 years.

This method of dog breeding produced the best pet and companion, being named Pomeranian for that area of Poland where it originated.

This dog with all of its intelligence, protected the Poles from the Prussian police, and would only eat Polish food prepared in the style of that Province. It was mainly a one person (one family) pet and companion.

When the regional harvest was completed, the root cellar filled, and the previous years wine fully aged, then the three day Polish weddings would be celebrated.

As the future bride and groom completed their home with the help of all the villagers, great anticipation was witnessed by the villager's conjecturing which couple would receive the smallest Pomeranian dog in the community, as one of their treasured wedding gifts.

This wedding gift would be a companion long after their children became adults, and would be at the anniversary when their hair began to turn silver (25th year of marriage).

In October of 1856, the lucky couple received their anticipated gift. Naming the Pomeranian dog *PIESEK*, being only nine months old, he spent his first night away from his mother in silence, at the new home of the honeymooning couple. It is claimed that *PIESEK* "minded" his own business, a trait of the Pomeranians, even when witnessing the "mass of confusion" of newly weds.

Ignacy and Frances were happy in their village, where Ignacy's occupation of a forester kept him away from home at times. *Piesek* was very intelligent, and even would wait for Frances outside the Church, knowing that Ignacy was away and *PIESEK* had the duty of protection.

On St. Stanislaus day, May 8, 1858 (a Saturday), Ignacy was awakened by Piesek. Piesek just returned with the village mid-wife, and at day-break Frances gave birth to an eight pound baby girl.

Mrs. Akuszerka, the mid-wife, informed Frances that the baby had the beauty of an angel. Since she was born on the feast of the Apparition of St. Michael, the Archangel, the baby should be named Michaline.

That Sunday, the visiting village born and raised ordained

Jesuit, baptized Michaline after the High Mass and in the presence of the entire congregation. Piesek kept his vigilance with Frances in the bedroom, but could not figure out why the new born was taken away so soon.

After the baptism, Piesek greeted all the relatives and villagers, as proud Ignacy served the aged brandy that remained from the 1856 wedding. Graciously and tenderly Ignacy served Frances a glass of brandy, then used for medicinal purposes. Whether Piesek got a lick of that brandy was never recorded.

The happy couple saved their gold coins, and in 1862 made reservations for passage to America in the spring of 1863.

There then was much planning for the voyage. The gold coins were sewed into certain items of clothing, which was a precaution for any "sharpies."

As the *samodzialka* (the homespun wool one piece covering) could be used for all, Frances made three extra ones, expecially for Michaline. Michaline was very spirited in playfully training her companion, Piesek, the obedience of silence.

The non-departing villagers all wanted ownership of Piesek. The village elders in their perfect elocution, pleaded the cause of the special treatment that awaited Piesek. Ignacy in his accepting the elder's vintage wine always stated that Frances is robust and enterprising, and Piesek was part of her wedding presents. Furthermore, Piesek and Michaline at this stage were inseperable, and Frances knew that the Pomeranian would be the first such dog in the Great Lakes area.

Travelling to the seaport was one of pleasure, as talkative Michaline was as silent as Piesek.

Boarding the passenger ship along the cold North Sea port, Michaline wore two large *samodzialkas'*. The inspecting officer smiled at Michaline, thinking the cold north wind was the reason for Michaline's attire. Not knowing that Piesek was under the *samodzialkas'*, Michaline's triumphal walk-up the gang-plank was evidenced by her eye-glance to her parents, as she knew that Piesek was on his way to America and of course, freedom from the "damned" Prussians.

With France's knowledge of languages, slim and lean in appearance, she walked passed the authorities at Castle Garden. Ignacy carrying Michaline, who tenaciously held the covered Piesek.

It is claimed that Piesek never barked until Coldwater, Michigan, was reached, where Ignacy was employed as a forester. The barking was Piesek's acknowledgment of the Polish chicken soup, which was not served on the Atlantic voyage.

SEQUEL

Ignacy was killed in a forest timber accident in 1866.

Piesek was taken to Northeastern Michigan in 1870, where Frances remarried and obtained a homestead.

In 1881, Piesek's double coat was silvery in color, and Frances continued to feed him the special chicken soup, with white meat finely cut. As each team of oxen or horses would pass the homestead cabin, Piesek's tiny ears would rise, awaiting a visit from Michaline, who now lived and was employed in Alpena, Michigan.

When Michaline exposed her fiance on one of her visits, Piesek gave his approval with the wagging of his still erect tail. Then back to the lamb-skin rug alongside the fireplace. Reminiscing and in his quick thinking, Piesek possibly thought that being at one honeymoon was sufficient.

In October, Michaline married in the village church, across the road from the homestead cabin. As the bride and groom departed from the Church the huge usually melodious church bells sounded "mystical." Frances claimed it was the sound of "I mourn death." To the village blacksmith, that sound reminded him of an old saying in France "God is advertising Himself."

As the musicians played "*PYTALA SIE PANNI, MLODEGO DOKTORA*" (The bride questioned the young doctor for advice), when Michaline was about to enter the cabin in preparation for another change of clothes, prior to the festivities, waves of tears rippled down her "cherry" red cheeks.

Frances immediately tried to comfort Michaline, and informed her not to worry by stating an old Polish proverb: *KTO SIE OZENI, TEN SIE ODMIENI*, which is, who gets married, changes for the better.

The tears were not because of the marriage, but by Michaline's extra sensory perception, prompted by the "mystical" sound of the huge church bells. Michaline knew that Prince Piesek, from the Palatine of Pomerania chose this day for his peaceful death at an advanced age.

Piesek knew that he defended all in time of battle, and thoughts of him did not perish in the tremendous day of death.

When this fact and fiction story was told, the convincing persuasive voice of the story teller was believed, and such story should be shared by all.

21
POLISH *POMIDORS*

As the early settlers in Michigan arrived from Poland during the height of the Civil War, a letter was written to Poland, returned to Michigan, and after all of these years it was translated into English.

These letters were written in the Gothic German script style but were written in Polish to confuse the Prussians. The Poles from that part of Prussian Poland could read and write in German and Polish in addition to writing in Latin which was common in that period of history.

The letter states:

Coldwater, Michigan
September 25, 1864

Dear Aniela,

Your youngest son Stanislaw is over two years old, so the gold coins enclosed are for his holyday gift, from the godmother.

Ignacy (husband) is working as a forester and employment is plentiful in Michigan due to the young men serving in the Union Army.

The vegetable garden is overabundant this year, and even this late, no frost as yet.

The apples were harvested, some stored, the others were pressed, and the cider and vinegar are presently fermenting.

When your sister departs for Michigan, she will board the train at Bromberg (Bydgoscz, Poland, presently) and travel to the harbor of Hamburg. The ship company has received the money for first-class passage to Quebec, due to the alleged blockade caused by the Civil War. From Quebec she will travel to Detroit, where we will meet her. Have Victoria bring this letter for confirmation and my complete address is also listed.

The tomatoes in this area are plentiful, but we do not have the *pomidor* variety. (It was alleged that the *pomidor* Polish variety had a taste of kielbasa in its flavored juices.)

Will write to the Prussian authorities to send me some of the pomidor variety seeds, but do not expect a reply as we rebelled against Prussianization prior to our departure early last spring; hence, the names of Wojtych and Pawlak are not conducive when dealing with the damned Prussians.

Your sister Victoria will be introduced to that young Polish forester she met at Sadki and whose parents still reside in Sadki (a small village near Bromberg). Have Victoria bring all of her wedding clothes, and she will stay with us until the marriage.

Victoria's *sznarowka* (corset in English; *korsett* in German; *gorset* in Polish, but *sznarowka* in high Polish) should be at least three in number for her many social participations that will precede her wedding day.

It is recommended that in Victoria's *sznarowka*, remove every other *podpierac* (stay), then the ocean passage will be one of relaxation in appropriate dress, not tied up like a Christmas goose ready for its destination.

By removing every other *podpierac* (stay), then such stay pockets could be filled by inserting your surplus *pomidor* (tomato) *nasiene* (seeds).

Ignacy and myself will meet Victoria at the Detroit port.

Since Victoria will leave from Bremen on St. Hedwig's Day, October 16, she should arrive in America before All Souls Day.

Victoria should use the German language here as Polish is only understood by some missionary priests and, of course, the numerous Poles and, of course, the Polish-speaking Prussians.

The visiting Jesuit missionary said Victoria could be married on *Andrzejki* Day. (It is a Polish custom that the popular maiden ladies have their fortunes told on the eve of this day.)

This day is prior to Advent (no marriages were allowed during Advent in that era of history).

The three-day wedding (a tradition and custom in Poland which was followed by the Poles in America until the beginning of the great war) will have roast ox, ham, cider, wodka, and, of course, *czarnina*, as we have a flock of geese. The home brew beer is very tasty in this area and I have two glasses a week with Ignacy.

My sister Michaline last week gave birth to a boy and they are going to baptize him Albert. As for myself, my second child will be born next spring, and with my luck it will be another girl.

Sincerely yours,

Frances

SEQUEL

Within a year after this letter was received and this letter being returned to Michigan by Victoria, Frances' forester husband was killed in the forest by a falling hardwood tree while inspecting and marking trees that were to be felled in the virgin forest in Branch County. Frances was a widow with two young daughters, and in that era of history there was neither ADC nor Social Security. Frances eventually married a widower with two sons, and they homesteaded in Presque Isle County.

Victoria arrived with her tomato-seed-stuffed corset. It was always alleged that those tomato seeds produced tomatoes having a kielbasa flavor.

It has been handed down to the sixth-generation Poles in

Michigan that if those original tomato seeds from Poland would have been perpetuated to date, such kielbasa-flavored tomatoes would be of two varieties today.

Yes, with and without garlic would be the two varieties.

These Poles had ingenuity to outsmart the oppressing Prussians; arrange transportation to Michigan for employment and marriage; but it is amazing how they brought the tomato seeds to Michigan. Fantastic and almost believable, the route of the seed.

But, shrewd Frances convinced Aniela that her godson Stanislaw should come to Michigan instead of being conscripted into the Prussian Army. Upon arriving in America Stanislaw was introduced to Frances' daughter Anna, and Frances responded with throwing another three-day wedding, this one in Posen, Michigan.

It being February 2, which is also Candlemas Day, the whole village was in church for the blessing of candles for the church and the home, then the wedding. Across the road from the church the whole village attended the wedding reception at Frances' homestead; however, there were no tomatoes served as tomatoes were not in season. The kielbasa was in the fresh style, smoked style, and dried cured style, but it has never been recorded whether these kielbasa styles had the two varieties, with garlic or without garlic, as the tomatoes that were imported to Michigan in three corsets. Yes, Polish humor and stories have been in the Great Lakes area since 1834.

22
THE PATRIOTIC POLE IN THE CIVIL WAR

"During the winter of 1863-64 the Second Cavalry of Michigan was constantly in the saddle, marching long distances, with most inadequate supplies and rations and clothing. The hardships and sufferings of the troops during the East Tennessee campaign had no parallel in the history of the war," according to the Record of Service, Michigan Volunteers in the Civil War.

The article continued: "The weather was cold, the snow often falling so as to cover the blankets of the men, who slept in the open air for want of tents. The only rations or forage issued was secured from the country by the soldiers themselves. The clothing had become worn by long use. It did not serve to protect the troops from the chilling rains and cutting winds. The horses were unfed and unshod, and the general suffering of the men and horses during the winter is one of painful contemplation."

Joseph Baranowski was a member of Company F, the Second Michigan Cavalry, and it stated that this Second Cavalry was in seventy major battles and had a 30% casualty list.

Baranowski enlisted on September 4, 1861, at Grand Rapids, Michigan (National Archives). The records state that he was mustered in on October 2, 1861. His enlistment records stated that he was born in the Kingdom of Poland and his occupation was a farmer and he was from Wright Township, Ottawa County, the State of Michigan.

This Second Cavalry achieved an enviable reputation in its stubborn fight with the enemy, driving the enemy in confusion from the field.

In December 1862 and January 1863 the Second Cavalry was in East Tennessee doing an immense amount of damage to the enemy's railroads and meeting the Confederates in the field on numerous occasions. In May 1863 this cavalry group was driven from the field by superior numbers and only escaped capture by the most heroic efforts.

In September 1863 they performed the most valuable service in holding the enemy's advance and scouting the country, giving important information to the Union commanders. After all of these battles and even under the most disheartening and discouraging circumstances, on the 29th of March, 1864, 326 members of this regiment re-enlisted for three years or during the war and returned to Michigan on a veteran furlough for thirty days. Among those that re-enlisted for three years was Joseph Baranowski, who stated in his re-enlistment; "I will bear true faith and allegiance to the United States of America."

Baranowski, in his service record of the Civil War obtained from the National Archives, further states that he re-enlisted at Mossy Creek, Tennessee. He had gray eyes, was 5′6″ tall, and was paid $60.00 for re-enlisting and was due for his period in the service the amount of $340.00. He was appointed bugler on January 5, 1864, for Company F of the Second Cavalry.

This regiment saw more battles than any other regiment from the State of Michigan. In 1864 they destroyed many of the wagons and captured the guns and baggage of the Confederate General Hood. During this year the Second Cavalry marched through Tennessee, Alabama, Kentucky, and Georgia, sustaining losses but inflicting much greater losses upon the enemy. On Christmas Eve, 1864, at the Pulaski, Tennessee, War Battle, Baranowski, a Pole, was at war in a Polish-named town, and there was no *oplatki* and *Cicha Noc* (wafers and Silent Night).

This regiment was splendidly organized and they had a very strict disciplinarian. As stated above, after engaging in 70 battles, they reached Macon, Georgia, on May 1, 1865, when the war was practically ended. The regiment was broken up into companies to guard a number of towns and preserve order. They were all mustered out on August 17, 1865, at Macon, Georgia, where they returned to Jackson, Michigan, where they were paid and disbanded on August 26, 1865.

Baranowski's muster-out roll reveals that he was paid a bounty of $210.00 plus an amount of $190.00 due him. After all of these battles, the Government charged this veteran $10.16 for losing one pair of pliers, one sabre belt and one screw driver.

After the war Baranowski went to his place of residence which presently is Marne, Michigan, which was in Wright Township, Ottawa County, and he purchased a farm.

On May 17, 1867, Baranowski married Helen Hodges of New York State and they had six children. The sixth child died in infancy, and his first wife in this childbirth. On August 28, 1882, Baranowski, a widower, was married to Catharine Rarajeczak at Conklin, Michigan, by Reverend Joseph Brueck at St. Joseph's Church. With this wife, the Patriotic Pole had five additional children (National Archives).

The hero of the Civil War, Baranowski arrived in Michigan at the age of 14 in 1854 with his father who was a forester. One of the main reasons that Baranowski's father left Poznan, Poland, was that he did not want to have his sons serve in the German Army (Affidavit, National Archives). Young Joseph Baranowski contacted his father in 1861 and his father stated, "You are of age–I cannot hold you back." Then young Joseph enlisted in the Civil War.

The National Archives reveal that in 1897 Baranowski was afflicted with "chronic catarrh" which affected his eyes and nose. At that time they gave Joseph Baranowski a pension. Baranowski died on March 22, 1924, then being 84 years of age and a retired farmer. After evaluating the complete records of twenty Polish-named soldiers from Michigan in the Civil War, Baranowski encountered the most battles and hence he was given the title "The MOST PATRIOTIC OF THE POLISH VETERANS from the State of Michigan in the Civil War."

23
WAR OF THE REBELLION HAS MICHIGAN-BORN POLES

Macomb County, Michigan, was well recovered from the "depreciated money of 1837" depression in the autumn of 1842. The residents of Clinton Township completed their abundant harvest. Food supplies were all stored in their "Michigan cellars," along with the apple cider which began to ferment in the small wooden casks. Such cider was to be used for medicinal purposes during the approaching winter months and also for festive occasions.

The engineer's pay of $66.67 per month would easily finance one of the "classier"homes in the then Village of Mount Clemens. Returning to such a home from his assistant engineering position on the Huron-Kalamazoo Canal project, Ludwik Wesolowski heard the cry of his first-born child. The midwife informed Ludwik Wesolowski that it was a boy. With joy he began serving the "hard cider," and following a Polish tradition he immediately named the boy Albert Z. (name, etc., census records 1850, July 31, on page 70, Clinton Township).

With this birth the new State of Michigan recorded the first person of Polish blood born within its boundary.

The 1860 census lists Albert's occupation as a surveyor. The year must have been traumatic for the youthful Wesolowski as his mother Sarah Jane (nee Fletcher) died on May 18 (Clinton Grove Cemetery tombstone).

It is assumed that young Albert assisted his father in land surveying in southeastern Michigan, with headquarters at Mount Clemens, until the hearing of the approaching "distant drums" of the Civil War.

Following his father's military training service footsteps, the National Archives reveal that "I, Albert Wesolowski, born in Mount Clemens, Michigan . . . by occupation a surveyor, do hereby acknowledge to have volunteered this 23rd day of July, 1862, to serve as a SOLDIER in the Army of the United States of America for a period of THREE YEARS, unless sooner discharged by proper authority; do also agree to accept such bounty, pay, rations, and clothing, as are, or may be, established by law for volunteers. And I, Albert Wesolowski, do solemnly swear, that I will bear true faith and allegiance to the United States of America, and that I will serve them honestly and faithfully against all their enemies or opposers whomsoever; and that I will observe and obey the orders of the President of the United States, and the orders of the officers appointed over me, according to the Rules and Articles of War." It was sworn and subscribed at Mount Clemens by the recruiting officer who was a lieutenant.

The examining surgeon testified that "I Certify on Honor that I have carefully examined the above-named volunteer agreeably to the General Regulations of the Army, and that in my opinion he is free from all bodily defects and mental infirmity, which would in any way disqualify him from performing the duties of a soldier."

Then with more bureaucracy in the forms, the recruiting officer had to Certify on Honor that he "minutely inspected . . . Albert Wesolowski prior to his enlistment . . . that he was entirely sober when enlisted . . . of lawful age." It concluded by stating "this soldier has light blue eyes, auburn hair, fair complexion, is 5′4″ high," and known as Corporal Albert Wesolowski.

Company F, 22nd Michigan Infantry, mustered on August 22, 1862, at Pontiac, Michigan. Upon arriving at the Detroit waterfront they ambarked for the Port of Cleveland. At Cleveland they were taken by railroad to Cincinnati, then to Covington, Kentucky, on their way to Lexington, Kentucky, where the company was afflicted with chronic diarrhea, and where many were confined here at the General Hospital.

The skirmishes and battles are mentioned in the Civil War books in any library, hence no detail of such skirmishes and battles.

The commanding captain of the company stated in June of 1863 that Corporal Wesolowski had been "unfit for duty . . . six months by reason of chronic diarrhea and general debility which totally unfits this soldier for service." The surgeon who examined Albert at enlistment was at Nashville, Tennessee, when Wesolowski received a "Certificate of Disability for Discharge" from the same doctor.

After he carefully "examined" the said soldier, the surgeon said "and find him incapable of performing the duties of a soldier because of chronic diarrhea and general debility and has not been able to discharge the duties of a soldier for the last six months, a part of which time he has been at the General Hospital, Lexington, Kentucky. In my opinion he will never be able to discharge the duties of a soldier," hence discharged on June 20, 1863, at Nashville (National Archives).

On orders of Major General Rosecrans, many of the soldiers from this regiment were discharged for this disease, which could have been caused from contaminated water. In fact, some of the soldiers who were in this company died from this ailment (National Archives Pension Records).

Upon returning to Michigan, Wesolowski farmed and was a surveyor while recuperating from the ailment.

Patriotism prevailed and Albert enlisted again on February 5, 1864, at Detroit, with the 8th Regiment of the Michigan Volunteers Cavalry for a period of three years. Mustered in at Detroit on February 15, 1864, the regiment left Grand Rapids, Michigan, on March 4, 1864, and served in Kentucky, Tennessee, and Georgia (National Archives).

During the Christmas season of 1864, Albert was on furlough at the Detroit Barracks (which was a hospital).

He was mustered out at Nashville, Tennessee, on September 22, 1865, being paid $300.00. He retained under G. O. No. 101, one revolver, $8.00; one Spencer carbine, $10.00; and one Sabre, $3.00.

Whatever Wesolowski did for a period of twenty years is a vacuum in the research, but in 1885 he was at the National Home (Soldiers Home), County of Milwaukee (Wauwatasa Township, Wisconsin).

The Act of June 27, 1890, provided that persons could be placed on the pension roll any person serving for the Union Army during the Civil War.

The resident of the National Home on July 10, 1890, filed a Declaration for Invalid Pension (National Archives). It stated that Wesolowski was "in the War of the Rebellion . . . served . . . honorably discharged." It continued that "he is totally unable to earn a support by reasons of chronic diarrhea and C & C; loss of teeth on account of scurvy and rheumatism and heart disease." It was further stated that "said disabilities are not due to vicious habits and to the best of his knowledge and belief permanent."

Another form requested of those receiving a pension was dated on February 15, 1898, wherein Wesolowski stated that he "never married and had no children." Nearest relative living is "Mrs. W. H. McGarvey, my sister, residence Port Gorlice, Galizien, *Oesterreich* or Austria." Albert did not know at the time that his wealthy sister Helena Jane died in December 1897 at Port Gorlice (now Gorlice, Poland). (From the *Multi-Millionaire* by NATSOLIM).

The Register of Deeds Office, Milwaukee County, Wisconsin, in Volume 173, page 301, lists a registration of death. Full name of the deceased, Albert Wesolowski; age, 57; birthplace, Michigan; single; date of death, September

16, 1899; cause of death, jaundice at the Hospital, National Home, Wisconsin. He is buried in Section 9, Grave 91, which is beneath an expressway overpass in Wood (Milwaukee), Wisconsin.

It is ironic that the first person of Polish extraction who was a soldier in the Civil War and was born in the State of Michigan in 1842 could not be buried in Michigan alongside his parents. Since 1870 there have been four vacant perpetual care spaces where his father Ludwik and Sarah Jane Wesolowski are buried. Their three children, all born in Michigan, are buried in Ontario, Wisconsin, and Galicia, Poland.

Being Polish, Albert must have been reminded many times by his military trained father of the old Polish proberb: "*Rybom woda, ludziom zgoda, bez, niej, nics*," a translation in essence being: "Water to fish, to men peace, without it, nothing," as the Poles were forced to fight Poles after the partition of Poland, and then American fought American in the War of the Rebellion.

24
THE FIRST MICHIGAN MULTIMILLIONARE

The first multi-millionaire in the Middle West was a woman. Helena Jane Wesolowski was born in 1845 at Pine and Market Streets (which is presently church-owned property) in the then Village of Mount Clemens, lot 9, section 10, as recorded in Liber M, page 230, the Macomb County records. She resided there according to the Macomb County census taken on July 31, 1850. The census of August 18, 1860, reveals that Helena Jane, then being 15 years of age, was a student. Education required, she was still in school approaching the age of 20, which was a rarity in the 1860's.

The 5′5″ (a tall woman for that era) auburn-haired, hazel-eyed beauty was married at the age of 22 on Wednesday, July 10, 1867, (Macomb County Marriage Records), to William H. McGarvey, a merchant from Petrolia, Ontario, where he owned "THE MAMMOTH STORE" (Lambton County Library, Wyoming, Ontario). The wedding ceremony was performed in Mount Clemens, Michigan, by Reverend H. E. Bissell, and the two witnesses were Augustus H. Canfield of Detroit, Michigan, and a James Williams of Mount Clemens. The festive wedding reception was held at her father's 5.6 acre estate, presently on North Avenue and Market Street in the City of Mount Clemens (*Polish Traditions* by NATSOLIM).

Immediately after the water voyage honeymoon, Helena went to Petrolia, Ontario, where she was of valuable assistance to her husband, who was elected reeve. Although her husband had a general country store, his "love" was oil wells. Within a year she and her husband had eighteen active oil producing wells, which started the wealth for the McGarvey family that ended when the Austrian and Russian Armies battled each other commencing in 1914.

In 1869 they had a daughter born in Petrolia, Ontario, whom they named Nellie. The census of 1871, on page 25, for the inhabitants of Petrolia, in the County of Lambton, Province of Ontario, lists Helena as being 25 years of age, the wife of an oil operator, a member of the Wesleyan Methodist Church, born in the United States, and her father being of Polish parentage (Archives, University of Western Ontario, London).

The Petrolia Centennial Book of 1966 devotes much space to Mr. McGarvey and explains the great wealth that was obtained by drilling for oil in the area. Although McGarvey operated a store, his chief interest was oil. He became an operator, later a refiner, rapidly developed into the leader of the oil industry, and he was part of "The Great Combination." This Great Combination consisted of a co-partnership agreement (illegal today) which was dated November 25, 1871, and called the Lambton Crude Oil Partnership. This group was composed primarily of producers and refiners and they manipulated the price of crude oil. In fact, after the Great Combination formation, the oil price was raised from $1.50 to $2.50 a barrel. With encouragement of Helena, her husband became the greatest in the oil drilling business and, in fact, he travelled to the wild western Canada for the Canadian Government to assess the potential oil fields.

The husband then went to Hanover in Germany to seek his first oil drilling operations in foreign areas. They were unsuccessful in Hanover, but they turned to Galicia, which is presently in Poland, and near the foothills of the Carpathian Mountains, oil was struck. They named the enterprise the *GALIZISHE-KARPATHEN* PETROLEUM *AKTIEN GESELLSCHAFT*, and this enterprise grew to tremendous proportions. Shortly after drilling, Galicia became the world's greatest oil producing fields and they established a refinery at Marionpol. They then constructed the largest refinery in the world at the Port of Trieste.

On July 6, 1876, the second daughter was born and they named her Mamie Helena. Having invested their money wisely, especially Helena with her collection of gold coins and bullion, the family was not affected by the depression of 1876.

In 1882 Helena with her two children arrived in the Imperial City, then known as the cultural center of the world, Vienna, in the Empire of Austria. As everyone knew, during the period of 1880 to 1898, Vienna was known for its elegance, enchantment, silk and diamonds. The new wealth was in Vienna and also the new industrialization. Between Vienna and her castle at Gorlice, Galicia, Helena enjoyed the lavish mood, the musical evenings, and also when they "threw" a monthly party. The life in Vienna was never serious, as there was a perpetual carnival time, continuous operas, and dancing under crystal chandeliers as the violins played. The only virtue known then was eat, drink, and be merry. The city was beautiful. It had hills with beech trees and meadows, and it was the most important trading center during the years before the turn of the century. As history records and repeats, titled persons married money people. Yes, Helena was possibly the wealthiest woman in the world, so her daughters were courted by nobility.

On November 12, 1896, at Vienna, her daughter Mamie Helena married Eberhard Friedrich Alexander Joseph Edward Graf von Zeppelin. This wedding was the most festive of the century's three-day weddings in Vienna (*Deutszches Adelsarchiv*, Marburg, West Germany).

Helena loved Vienna, but for peace and tranquility, and also because it reminded her of her youth in Michigan and Canada, she spent most of her time in her castle at Port Gorlice, Galicia. This castle was along the river, so she must have thought of her childhood days in Mount Clemens, Michigan, where her father was an engineer on the Huron-Kalamazoo Canal, which Canal was never completed, and then her father was elected to the important position of County Surveyor.

As the most beautiful and mild autumn in the memory of the residents of the Carpathian foothills drew to a close in 1897, Countess Mamie Helena Graf von Zeppelin, with her sister Nellie, went to their mother's castle in Gorlice, and in December of that year Helena Jane Wesolowski, the woman from Mount Clemens, Michigan, died in her mammoth castle along the canal.

It is ironic that Helena Jane Wesolowski, the first multi-millionaire from the Middle West, is buried in the country of her father's birth, where the wealth was found, in the country that he loved. The father was deported by Austria after the Warsaw Insurrection. He in turn is buried in the city of her birth.

Yes, the old Polish proverb prevailed, "*Pod dobra gwiazda sie urodzila*," meaning, she was born under a good star.

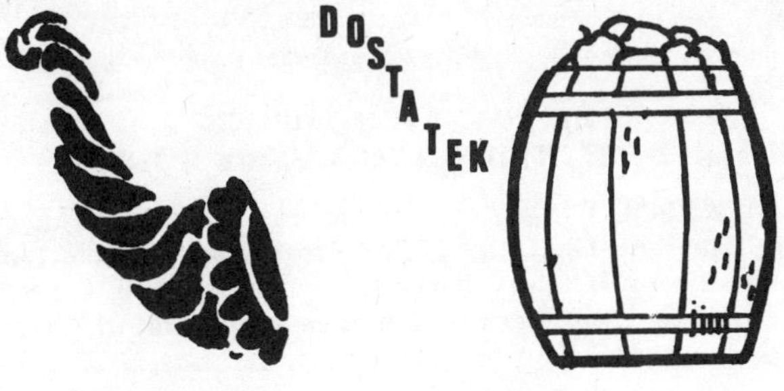

**THE TOMBSTONE OF THE
FIRST ELECTED SLAVIC OFFICE HOLDER**

LUDWIK WESOLOWSKI was an engineer on the defunct Huron-Kalamazoo Canal in 1838. In 1850 Wesolowski was elected to the important position of County Surveyor under the Whig Party.

The tombstone is in Section A of beautiful Clinton Grove Cemetery, Cass Avenue, Mt. Clemens, Michigan.

CERTIFIED COPY OF RECORD OF MARRIAGE

STATE OF MICHIGAN, County of Macomb, Mt. Clemens, Michigan, } ss. RECORD NUMBER ______

I, Edna Miller, Clerk of the County of Macomb and of the Circuit Court thereof, the same being a Court of Record having a Seal, do hereby certify that the following is a copy of the Record of Marriage, now remaining in my office, and of the whole thereof, viz:

Bridegroom		Bride	
Full Name of Bridegroom	WILLIAM H. McGARVEY	Full Name of Bride	HELENA WESOLOWSKI
City, Residence, State	Petrolia, Ontario, Canada	City, Residence, State	Mt. Clemens, Michigan
Age	23	Age	22
Color	--	Color	--
Times Previously Married		Times Previously Married	
Birthplace-City and State	--	Birthplace-City and State	--
Occupation	--	Occupation	
Father's Full Name	--	Father's Full Name	--
Mother's Maiden Name	--	Mother's Maiden Name	--

U.S. Revenue Stamp 5¢ Canceled

Date of License	Date of Marriage	Place of Marriage	Magistrate or Clergyman	Official Title
July 10, 1867	July 10, 1867	Mt. Clemens, MI	H.N. Bissell	Minister

Witnesses to Marriage — Names	Residences
Augustus H. Canfield	Detroit, Michigan
James Wiliams	Mt. Clemens, Michigan

In Testimony Whereof, I have hereunto set my hand and affixed the seal of said Circuit Court, this 11th day of March A.D. 1976-

SEAL

EDNA MILLER Clerk.

By [signature] Deputy Clerk.

MC-67

"THE NICKEL PARLEY"

Five cents for the marriage license revenue stamp was parlayed into multimillions. Within one year this couple had eighteen producing oil wells at Petrolia, Ontario.

Vienna eventually was the headquarters of William and Helena. They entertained the aristocracy, royalty and military. Helena was considered the wealthiest woman in the world in 1895.

A vivacious daughter, Mamie Helena, married a von Zeppelin in 1896 at Vienna. In that period of history Vienna was considered the "playground" of the universe.

25
BRONSON, MICHIGAN, POLES

Many of the Poles who eventually settled in Alpena and Presque Isle County, Michigan, came from Branch County, Michigan, during the lumber "boom" and the homesteading days.

During the Civil War and after the Insurrection of 1863 in Poland, plus the tyranny of the Prussians, the Poles immigrated to Michigan, some even by way of Quebec.

These Poles arrived by railroad at Coldwater, Michigan, and settled in a town called Bronson, Michigan. (U.S. Census Report, 1870). In fact, the writer's paternal grandmother was born in Coldwater, Michigan, in 1865, which had a substantial Polish population.

The Poles were a very religious group and when first arriving in Coldwater, there was no church. On certain days they would all travel to Hillsdale, Michigan, for the Latin Mass.

In 1867 a priest from Holland, a Father Cornelius Korst, who had knowledge of the German and Polish languages (The Poles knew German), started a mission Church in Bronson. These devout Poles named the church in honor of the Assumption of the Blessed Mother. It is to be known that the church records were all destroyed by fire so the marriage, baptism, and death records are no longer in existence.

One of the missionaries to Bronson, Michigan, in 1870 was Father Francis Xavier Schulak, a Jesuit, who arrived in the Middle West in 1865 (*The Sailing Missionary* by Natsolim, unpublished.)

The census records of Branch County of 1870 list many families that eventually settled in Alpena and Presque Isle Counties.

Many parishes that have a heavy concentration of Poles have named their Church St. Mary. This is due to the Polish heritage of the patron Saint of Poland, who is the Blessed Mother.

26
POLISH BAGELS
(*BAJGEL*–SILESIAN STYLE)

When the Poles came to the Great Lakes area one of their foods was the bagel.

The bagel was originated in Vienna, Austria, by Jan Sobieski's cook, and the Polish cook named them *bajgel*.

As history records, Sobieski began his Battle of Vienna against the Turks on September 12, 1683 to save Christianity and Europe.

After a few encounters in the battle, Sobieski obtained all the camels, mules, oxen and sheep. Were they served with bagels?

The recipe for the Silesian-style bagel is:

4 tablespoons melted lard, or bacon grease, or goose grease, or butter. (An oil can be used by vegetarians.)
2 tablespoons beet sugar
½ teaspoon coarse salt
1 cup of lukewarm well water
½ ounce of dried yeast
2 small eggs, or one duck egg
1 pound flour

Mix the lard, sugar and salt with the water thoroughly, then stir in the yeast. Add beaten eggs, then mix in the flour. Let rise, then drop in the boiling rain water. After rising in the boiling rain water, place on buttered baking tin and bake for thirty minutes at 375°.

The exact date when bagels arrived in America is not known. However, with their usage in Pomeranian Danzig, these bagels were placed on sailing vessels out of the Port of Danzig which supplied the ships not only with bagels–or as we would call it today hardtack–but also with salted herring, such herring being obtained by the Polish fisherman of the Baltic Sea. These herring were considered the best in all of the European countries.

27
ZAJAC ZUPA

The Polish title of this chapter means rabbit soup.

Most of the early Poles in Michigan were foresters who had skill in snaring rabbits and other wild animals. Food got scarce during the Civil War. In the 1860's to 1896, chickens in Michigan were raised for their eggs. Only the old hens and surplus roosters met their fate in the soup pot.

This soup could be made a variety of ways. A creamed broth of the rabbit soup was fed to the infants. Adults would carry the meat of the rabbit with their Polish bagels in their knapsacks when out in the forest for their lunch and snacks. Beef, pork and the meat of the animals of the wild were a common food, but rabbit served as a dual-purpose delicacy.

In preparing this soup usually three rabbits were used, as Polish families were large in America. In Poland the families were small.

The ingredients for the rabbit soup were:

2 to 3 lbs. cut-up rabbit

3 quarts of water

2 bay leaves

a dash of *marijonka* (marjoram)

1½ cups diced potatoes

1 cup sliced carrots

a dozen parsley sprigs, if available

1 cup onion (wild onions were preferable, especially in April)

a dash of dill, or dill seed
1 cup chopped celery, if in season
1 cup parsnips, chopped
½ lb. salt pork
½ pint of cream
3 oz. of flour

Take the cut-up rabbit and soak in water and vinegar for 24 hours to bleach the flesh.

Boil rabbit in cold water for about one hour, then add the vegetables, the seasoning, and the diced salt pork.

Simmer until the rabbit is almost overtender, that is where the meat is falling away from the bone. Add water if necessary. Separate the meat from the bones. Set aside some meat and broth for other uses.

Blend the flour with the cream and stir into the soup.

Bring to a boil, stirring continuously until the soup has thickened and is smooth.

This soup can be served with bagels or bread, noddles or boiled potatoes.

Realizing that the ingredients are very expensive with today's food prices, a person should at least have one of these meals to realize what our ancestors had as a delicacy during the Civil War period here in the State of Michigan.

Furthermore, the winter of 1870-71 was severe, and many homesteaders existed on rabbits, bagels, and the abundant supply of fish, as their supplies were exhausted, but saved by the rabbit from starvation.

28
RZEZNIK MEAT MARKET

Rzeznik is a butcher in Polish, so when the first Pole opened his meat market in Bronson, Michigan, in 1869, the non-Polish speaking area residents would purchase his *kiszka.*

So, Jacob Pawlak was known in the area as Mr. Rzeznik (Razznik phonetically). Being owner of a meat market around Bromberg (Bydgoscz presently) in Prussian Poland, Jacob's sisters Michaline and Frances convinced Jacob to come to Michigan.

Upon arriving in Michigan in 1867 Jacob worked for butchers in the Coldwater area. Within two years the economizing Pawlak had his own business in the Polish area of Bronson and a good command of the English language so he began advertising.

Typical of his ads were:

Dealers in all Kinds of Fresh, Salt, and Smoked Meats, Lard, Tallow, etc. . . .

Below followed with:

Cash Paid for Pork, Beef, Lard, Tallow, Hides and Sheep Pelts

All of the goose feathers and down were shipped to Chicago to a pillow maker. It is said that Mr. Razznick, with his pleasant personality, made more money from the feathers than he did in the meat market.

During the early 1870s, Jacob in his monthly trips to Chicago met a beautiful brown-eyed butcher's daughter. As the Poles were arriving in masses in Chicago, Jacob established a meat market in Chicago, married the butcher's daughter, and this merger can be considered the first Polish father-in-law and son-in-law partnership in the Great Lakes area.

29
THE WATER WELL MYSTERY

The National Archives land records of the Polish homesteaders in Michigan, reveal in the certification that in 1870 all of the drinking water wells were 12 feet deep.

Was this depth of their wells based on superstition or their deep religious beliefs? This is a mystery, as water was available at depths from four feet to 20 feet in that farming area.

Some theories are listed, so the reader must form his own deduction. In Poland, Copernicus said that there are 365 days per year. At the Polish measurement of 3.65 meters, it equalled 12 feet in America.

At 3.65 meters in Poznan and Pomerania, the water wells were sweet and sufficient.

There are 12 apostles, and they were on water! A cord of wood is 4 X 8, which equals twelve, as the homesteaders were formerly foresters. The rotation of the earth on a yearly basis provides 12 hours of daylight and 12 hours of darkness, and many of the homesteaders were near the 45th parallel. From Cancer to Capricorn and back to the zenith of Cancer it takes 12 months. Did the Lord choose 12 apostles, because of the 12 months? Man's best animal friend, the dog, reaches maturity at 12 months.

Did some village astronomer say: "we cannot use meters here, so the 3.65 meters is 12 feet, and with the Apostles blessing, all wells in this area will be twelve feet?"

This mystery was never solved, and cannot be considered folklore. Possibly the solution to this mystery is in the Archives of Poland?

30
THE FIRST POLISH FAMILIES IN ALPENA

Although there were Polish people in Michigan in 1820, mass immigration of Poles to Michigan occurred in 1854. The first two Polish families who settled in Alpena, Michigan, came directly from Poland which, in itself, is unique. The first Pole located in Fremont (Alpena) was there in 1858, a single man, about whom I have written in another article.

John Potter, the census taker in Alpena in 1870, listed on page 59, June 18, 1870, two Polish neighbors, as follows:

A. The household of Stephen Wellington, age 32, who works in a sawmill, resides with his wife, Catherine, age 22, their daughter, Mary, age one, all born in Poland.

B. The household of Jacob Bromcosk, age 29, who works in a sawmill, residing with his wife, Helen, age 27, and their two daughters, Susan, age 4, and Victoria, age 1, all born in Poland.

With surnames such as these, one wonders if they are Polish. They probably were descendants of sixteenth century Scotsmen who immigrated to the democratic Kingdom of Poland because of religious strife and depression in the British Isles. These people quickly became Polanized but, as in any democracy, they retained their original surnames.

The names Stephen, Catherine and Mary are common given names in Poland, thus Mr. Wellington became a Polanized Scotsman because his ancestors settled in Poland.

Mr. Bromcosk's name was mispelled by the census enumerator, who attempted to Anglicize the first Polish name he encountered. The given names, Jacob, Helen and Victoria, are also commonly used in Poland. Many Polish girls are named Zosia, which, during that era of history were listed as "*Sosia*" possibly derived from Susan.

The first massive groups of Poles visiting Alpena in 1868 and 1869 were on their way to Crawford's Quarry to seek employment as foresters at the Rogers and Molitor Company. In 1870 they disembarked at False Presque Isle Harbor, on Lake Huron, heading for their newly acquired 160-acre homesteads, located in the area of St. Casimir's Church, in the present Posen and Pulaski Townships, which they obtained for the sums of fourteen dollars each.

Other persons listed in the 1870 Alpena census had Polish first names such as Sophia, Amelia, Kasper, Matthias, Antony and various others, with their birthplace noted as Prussia. Because Prussia took possession of *Wielka Polska* (Great Poland) in 1795, the censuses taken in 1860, 1870, and 1880 list the Pole's birthplace as Prussia instead of Poland as the censuses of 1840 and 1850 indicate. The surname Comstock, one of the prominent Michigan names, appears in the census list also. The only other community listed in the Alpena County census in 1870 is Ossineke.

According to the census report, the main occupation listed was working in a sawmill, with all single men residing in a boarding house. Most of the textile merchants and peddlers in Alpena during that period were also born in Poland but were not of Slavic blood. The records in the National Archives indicate that other Poles arrived in Alpena and Presque Isle County in 1870 from Branch, Ottawa, Bay and Wayne County, Michigan, and from Saint Joseph's and Noble Counties in Indiana.

As the early Polish settlers in Michigan became assimilated into the general society by intermarriages, our computerized extension figures show that Polish blood exists in about four and a half million Michigan people today. It is no wonder then that one of the favorite Polish traditional foods, *kielbasa* (sausage), is so popular despite its relatively high cost, attracting brisk sales among all Slavs. Polanized Scots, wearing their traditional plaids, are often seen purchasing this treat and delicacy, a taste they acquired from their ancestors who were introduced to it in Michigan over one hundred fifty-five years ago.

VIEW of ALPENA, MICHIGAN— 1865
FIRST BRIDGE IN CONSTRUCTION
—ALPENA NEWS

31
POLISH PEAS

In the northern part of Poland, in the province of Pomerania and Poznan, after the leaf lettuce was picked, the next vegetable available could be termed snow peas.

When the Poles left their native provinces and settled in south-western Michigan, all of their gardens were planted with peas because this was an early crop and after the peas were picked a different vegetable could be grown in the same location.

There were numerous recipes for peas but when the Poles moved to northeastern Michigan and homesteaded their farms commencing in 1870, they made a special delicacy which was served in season.

At about the same time the green peas were mature, it was time to send the lambs out to pasture after such lambs were milk fed, usually until June. Certain of these lambs had to be consumed for food because the lambs provided meat, and the hides of such lambs were treated and eventually made into vests, rugs for the homestead floors, and, of course, baby booties.

At the time the lambs were butchered for food and nutrition the green peas were ripe and from this came the favorite delicacy known as Polish pea-and-lamb soup. The recipe called for four pounds of lamb shank and two pounds of lamb breast (or the same amount of meaty lamb bones). Add sufficient water and cook until almost tender and the beginning of the formation of broth. Add twelve finely chopped green onions (especially wild onions), otherwise two whole onions chopped; dried celery leaves; four teaspoons of butter.

Sauté the onions and the celery leaves and add three pounds of pod young green peas. After sautéing, add more water and add into the soup. Cook until done. Different types of seasoning if available could be added, such as a dash of salt and a dash of sugar.

The reason the spring lambs had to be butchered was strictly for necessity as a food because usually in June the geese and chickens were moulting and when any fowl are in their period of moulting, it is not recommended that they be consumed for food.

Any homesteader only had a certain amount of pasture land and it was thought in that period of history that the sheep and lambs would eat the grass almost to its roots thereby not allowing the cattle to graze on such land. Whatever the reason for such thinking of the homesteaders has never been recorded, but they raised enough lamb to provide food for them and, of course, as previously stated, they needed the hides which had many uses.

It is amazing how the homesteaders had everything in season and the amount of planning that was required for a balanced diet, and stored in their root cellars.

At this time of history wherein all of the homesteaders ate the foods in season, it is not amazing that the obituary column and the death certificates of the homesteaders reveal "died of old age," (County Clerk Records, Presque Isle, Michigan), and many of them well into their eightieth birthdays, more than double their life expectancy of forty years when they were born in Northern Poland.

32
POZNAN PROVINCE WINE

In the meadows of Poland, especially in the Province of Poznan, the dandelions were identical to the variety found in Michigan.

This was noticed by the Poles who came in masses in 1854 to 1865 to Michigan, hence, their first wine was obtained from the dandelion.

At that time of history, they realized that dandelion wine had many curative factors: neuralgia, liver tune-up, gastric stomach, and its use in moderation would lead to an active golden age.

Such wine would cure spring fever, as every one had to pick the dandelions. It was another method of keeping the children of the homesteaders busy, as the Polish people believed in training their young early in life, as the Poles were always known as good workers.

During the shortage of provisions during the Civil War, the Polish homesteaders made their own dandelion wine and other liquors for the holidays and festivities. Since these Poles could read and write Polish and German, many of them brought this recipe from Poland.

A whittling knife was used to remove the whole dandelion plant. Then the whole head would be cut off. The rest of the plant and stalk was fed to the chickens and geese; especially the clucking hens, whose activities at this time of the year kept them on the nest where they required extra nutrients.

Polish children, with their flexible fingers, would remove the petals of the dandelion flower. Surplus heads were fed to the pigs by the senior citizens, who always pitched in for the occasion.

At times the dandelion greens would be used for a salad, as the northern leaf lettuce was only in its initial growth. The dandelion greens could also be wilted in bacon grease and bacon *skorki* (skins).

After the petals were picked, they would have to be washed at least three times to remove any grit and dirt.

Two quarts of dandelion petals were placed in a loose cloth, and laid across the bottom of a crock small enough to permit the cloth to over-lap the upper edge of the crock.

Pour one gallon of boiling rain water (no minerals) over the flower petals and soak for at least five days. Stir each day, after the daily chores are completed. Remove any surface mold that forms. Keep the crock covered with cloth or a board (the board that kept the saurkraut packed or the dill pickle fermenting board).

At the end of five days, remove cloth and strain the juices to remove any impurities.

Warm the juice (liquid) and stir in two pounds of sugar, stirring until the sugar is completely dissoved. Within 24 hours, after the liquid is cool, add one half ounce of yeast and blend in the yeast. Cover with a cloth and let ferment for two weeks or fourteen days.

When completely fermented, pour into bottles and cap with corks.

This dandelion wine was made in huge quantities, usually three times during the month of May. Sunshine was hot enough to fully open up the flowers in May, and dandelions could be relied upon to appear every year.

The first batch of wine was tested and used on the 4th of July celebration, which the Poles observed by recollecting Pulaski and Kosciousko in their role during the Revolutionary War. It was then served on August 15, the day set aside for the flowers to be blessed in Church, a tradition of Poland followed by the Polish Americans.

The wine was then stored until after harvesting of the crops. Then after the first Sunday in October, all of the community would donate their wine to the bride and groom for the three day wedding. It should be noted that each day of the wedding party, at least one oxen was roasted, in addition to the other foods as *czarnina* (duck soup), fresh kielbasa, roast goose, breakfast ham, apple sauce and potatoes, plus the bread and freshly churned butter. The desserts were apple pie, baked apples, and pears in syrup, which were all in season. Not much wine was consumed at these feasts.

The three day weddings were discontinued during the Great War. The making of dandelion wine continued until May, 1933, at which time it was evident that the Prohibition Act would be repealed, it then became cheaper to purchase a commercially produced wine.

Like the rest of the third generation Polish American children born in Michigan, the writer was happy to see the Prohibition repealed. This meant that dandelion plants were picked only for the clucking hens, and picking required only half the time formerly necessary. The leisure time could be spent fishing, kite flying, or going into the forests in beautiful North Eastern Michigan. Then in the evening instead of picking petals, the writer would stop to visit the librarian who always had an abundant supply of licorice candy, which candy was consumed while browsing the books stacks. Then to the Boys Club for further activities.

33
POLISH *SKLEP* (CELLAR)

Sklep in archaic Polish is a vault. Such vault had other various names but the one used in Michigan was the root cellar which in essence was an underground storage compartment.

As most of the early Polish settlers to Michigan came from a Northern climate, namely near the town of the present Bydgoscz, which is on the 53rd degree parallel north in latitude and in the area of Biskupin where it was stated that Biskupin was the first Polish settlement in the world. Food storage was a problem as in the year 800 there were no refrigerators.

Since the Poles that arrived in Michigan were lumbermen and foresters and had a knowledge of working with wood, assembling the root cellar was very easy as they constructed such root cellars in Poland. Such cellar was usually constructed at the highest land elevation about fifty yards from the homesteader's cabin. The hole was dug into the ground. The cellar measured ten by twenty feet. Huge logs were notched at the ends to fit into each other. They were laid on top of each other and evenly matched. The cellars were built due north and south because of the snow from the north and northwest in that latitude.

The inside walls and the floor would be lined with huge planks. Both wood slats facing north were removed during the spring when the dry north wind would blow. When the log cellar was completed, it was covered with earth and a layer of sod.

The people in that time of history averaged only 5′4″

tall, and the cellar from sand floor to ceiling was only five feet high.

Although there were no rats or other rodents (the hogs ate all the garbage), these cellars had to be of heavy structure because there were weasel, mink, wolf, fisher and foxes.

The homesteaders, who were farmers and foresters, would store carrots, potatoes, cabbage, turnips, rutabaga and other vegetables in those cellars. In the autumn, the russet and Ben Davis apples were stored there.

During the spring and summer months the foresters would also use this cellar for their milk, butter, and cream.

Various types of meats would be stored in these cellars such as cured, smoked, dried ham and bacon and a sausage made mainly of beef which would cure itself and would dry itself which today could be compared to hard salami.

After the chickens were introduced in the 1870's, National Archives Records even revealed the number of chickens per homesteader, any surplus of eggs would be stored in the cellar in crocks. Such eggs would be placed in crocks; a layer of eggs, then one layer of coarse salt, continuing in this manner until the crock was filled. These eggs were used during the autumn of the year when the hens laid fewer eggs.

As a youngster the writer would go into these root cellars, especially when visiting a relative on the farm, and as any child's imagination he thought that he was visiting the catacombs of Europe. It was very cool, but the amazing part of the root cellars is that they were constructed in the year of 1870 and were still in use in the year of 1960. So the question remains that with all the various energy shortages it makes a person wonder if we should revert back to using the root cellar as it would have a two-fold purpose: There would be no cost of electrictiy, and food could be stored in quantity in the event of any emergency.

34
THE FIRST POLISH HOMESTEADER'S WIDOW

An affidavit sworn and subscribed on the 17th day of June, 1876, by the County Clerk of Presque Isle, with the Seal of the Circuit Court, reveals one of the many tragedies of the first homesteaders.

After the customary formalities, the National Archive records, revived a century later, stated in this affidavit: "Michaline Witucki, being duly sworn, deposes and says that her husband, Franz Witucki, who took up the within homestead, was killed by the fall of a tree while chopping wood on his homestead on the third day of February, 1871, and that since then I and my children have continued to live upon and work said homstead." It was signed by her mark as Michaline Witucki.

In addition to the affidavit the final proof required under the Homestead Act of May 20, 1862, in essence said proof said that August and Lorenz Kowalksi do solemnly swear that they have known Michaline Witucki for six years past and that she is the wife of the late Franz Witucki and head of a family consisting of four children, and her husband had declared his intention to become a citizen of the United States, that she is an inhabitant of the southeast ¼ of Section 9 in Township No. 33 North, range No. 6 East, and that no other person resided upon the said land entitled to the right of homestead or pre-emption.

It continues by stating that the said Franz Witucki entered upon and made settlement on said land on the 18th day of October 1870, and has built a house thereon 20 × 14′

shingle roof, one outside door, three windows, and comfortable to live in, and she had lived in said house and made it her exclusive home from the second day of November 1870 to the present time, and that she has since said settlement ploughed, fenced and cultivated about ten acres of said land and has made the following improvements, to wit, built a barn 18′ X 25′. It was witnessed and signed by Lorenz Kowalski who was the stalwart on the 17th day of June 1876.

Franz Witucki of Noble County, Indiana, filed his Application No. 839 on August 20, 1870, at Detroit, Michigan, along with his brother-in-law, Matthias Scheminsky, and another friend, a Valentine Muchynski. Each of the three homesteaders obtained 160 acres of land, which presently frontages M-65, at a cost of only $14.00. At the time of making such application, it stated, "It is required of the homestead settler that he shall reside upon and cultivate the land embraced in his homestead entry for a period of five years from the time of filing the affidavit, being also the date of entry. An abandonment of the land for more than six months works a forfeiture of the claim. Further, within two years from the expiration of the said five years he must file proof of his actual settlement and cultivation, failing to do which his entry will be cancelled."

The final affidavit was issued on June 27, 1876, wherein Michaline Witucki, widow of Franz Witucki (deceased), made a final affidavit. She further stated that "my husband during his lifetime declared his intention to become a citizen of the United States and that I with my husband made actual settlement upon and have cultivated said land, having resided there since the date of entry to the present time."

As with any government agencies, the Detroit Land Office was confused, so Michaline Witucki, the widow, had to go to Rogers City, wherein the County Clerk, Frederich

Denny Larke, filed another affidavit on August 12, 1877. This affidavit, with the seal of a Circuit Court, stated Michaline Witucki, being duly sworn, doth depose and say that she is the widow of Franz Witucki, who located as a government homestead the southeast quarter of Section 9, T-33N, R6E, Michigan; that Franz Witucki was her husband, true and correct name; and that her true and correct name is Michaline Witucki; that she has not married since the death of her husband but has constantly resided and does now reside on said homestead and requests that the United States may have a patent issued to her, Michaline Witucki, as widow of Franz Witucki. It was signed her mark with Michaline Witucki.

This affidavit was sent to the Land Office at Detroit wherein the Register on August 8, 1877, stated I hereby certify according to an affidavit made by Michaline Witucki that the correct spelling of the name is Witucki agreeing within certificate.

Michaline's neighbor to the north was her sister Frances (nee Pawlak) Wojtych Scheminsky (Szymanski).

It sure was a tragedy for Michaline when after three months after the completion of their homestead cabin her husband Franz was killed on his own property.

Michaline having a neighbor, a sister, the sister along with her husband and the children of both helped on the farm.

Michaline's daughter Agnes married a Peter Gappa who was given part of the farm and undoubtedly helped support the widow. Michaline eventually sold a portion of her property. It should be noted that the original cabin built by these homesteaders is still in existence in Posen, Michigan. This cabin is over 100 years of age, and possibly an historical marker should be granted to the Witucki and Szymanski homesteads.

The homesteaders going into this very rugged environment were psychologically and physically durable. Therefore, even though they witnessed many tragedies, they fulfilled their dream—the dream of owning a huge farm in America.

35
CABIN TO COFFIN

Polish people are very practical in regard to life and death. This practicality is from an old Polish proverb which says: "*Smierc i zona od Boga Preznaczona*," which translated means "Death and wife are destined by God."

When the forests in southwestern Michigan and the northern part of Indiana were nearing the point of depletion, the Poles from Branch and St. Joseph Counties, Michigan, and from Noble, LaPorte, and St. Joseph Counties, Indiana, heard that they could obtain homestead land in Northeastern Michigan, they immediately took the railroad trip to Detroit. At the Detroit Land Office they obtained 160 acres of land for $14.00 (in gold coins), such land being situated in the present Presque Isle County, Michigan.

One of the homesteaders, Frank Witucki, along with his wife, two sons and two daughters, made settlement in Presque Isle County (Section 9, present Posen, Michigan, along M-65), and on October 18, 1870, his homesteader's cabin was completed. That fall and winter was the worst winter recorded in that part of Northeastern Michigan.

According to the land records at the National Archives Office, Washington, D.C., in an affidavit filed by the homesteader's widow (wife), Michaline Witucki, it stated that on February 3, 1871, Frank Witucki was killed by "fall of a tree while chopping wood on his homestead." The then widow Michaline had a sister who resided in the same section to the north which was one half mile away and presently is the property across the street from the Polish Church in Posen, Michigan. One mile to the north of the Witucki cabin was the Mushynski cabin and across the road in section 3, which is presently alongside M-65,were the cabins of the community stalwarts, one Lawrence Kowalski and Frank Roshek.

The community homesteaders had signal with the farm bells, so immediately the other homesteaders began either walking or on their oxen-drawn sleighs in the heavy and cold "mountainous" snow and with their homesteading determination, durability, and ruggedness knew what the procedure would be to bury the first homesteader since the area was composed mostly of Poles. This was the first Polish *Pusto Noc* (which in essence means "the empty night" or "the person would be missed").

The (a)wake was held on Saturday evening and the adjoining homesteaders brought their rationed supplies plus the rabbits and other foods trapped by the farmers-foresters, trying to establish a new homestead.

That Saturday evening the prayers were alternated between an eighteen-year-old and the deceased's sister-in-law, Frances (nee Pawlak) Wojtych Scheminsky.

They would say the complete rosary and practically all of the known litanies as there was no spiritual advisor stationed in the then remote Presque Isle County.

The *PUSTO NOC* and the prayers would start with "In the name of the Father, and of the Son, etc.," plus the Apostles' Creed and the fifteen chief mysteries. The "Our Father" would be stated on the larger beads and the "Hail Mary" on every small bead, and each decade of the rosary was terminated with "Glory be to the Father, etc."

These Poles realized during these lengthy rosaries that a grave would have to be dug. The Polish men dug a grave and they, being skilled in woodworking as they were foresters, made a coffin from the pinewood that surrounded them in the virgin forests.

The men in the process of digging the grave and building a coffin, left the women and children to recite the prayers at the *Pusto Noc*. The reciter commenced with the first part of the Holy Rosary which was the five joyful mysteries:

1. The Annunciation
2. The Visitation
3. The Nativity
4. The Presentation
5. The Finding of the Child Jesus in the Temple

The second part of the rosary consisted of the five sorrowful mysteries:

1. Prayer and Bloody Sweat in the Garden
2. The Scouraging at the Pillar
3. The Crowning with Thorns
4. The Carrying of the Cross
5. The Crucifixion

Usually the third part of the rosary was recited by the eighteen-year old in order that he complete the third part and complete the full rosary. He would recite the five glorious mysteries:

1. The Resurrection
2. The Ascension
3. The Descent of the Holy Ghost
4. The Assumption
5. The Crowning of the Blessed Mother

Then one of the stalwarts of the community, usually a man, would start the Litany of the Blessed Mother. This would continue, but when it was said "*Krolowa Korona Polski*," which would mean in essence "The Crown Queen of Poland," there would be a pause of silence, as all of these homesteaders knew and still admired the Patron Saint of Poland. After the litanies were concluded, the people in attendance ate their meager rations and awaited the graveside service at daybreak.

What member of this Polish homesteading community

said the prayers at the graveside is not known and has never been recorded; However, from all indications it was either Frank Roshek, Lawrence Kowalski, or Matthias Scheminsky (Szymanski). The durable, rugged and determined Witucki was buried on his homestead, as no cemetery existed in this recent homesteading community according to the information that was handed down verbally from generation to generation of Poles in that area of northeastern Michigan.

These homesteaders being from the area of Poland which is along the border of Pomerania and Poznan were always very practical and they had many proverbs that were used in that area of Poland exclusively, and the people in attendance possibly realized that the colloquialism "*po smierci dupa nie rzadzi*" (which in essence means that after you die your butt does not rule and it can be buried anywhere).

This *Pusto Noc* must have been one of sorrow as these Poles departed from the Prussian tyranny in Pomerania, were happily employed as foresters in Coldwater, Michigan, then along the Michigan and Indiana border for a few years in a reforestration program, then to the Detroit Land Office.

From the Detroit Land Office to Presque Isle County to the present Village of Posen (then unnamed) and then one of their group from the happy completion of his homestead cabin to his coffin in only fifteen weeks. This same mysterious number being 15 which 15 is in the Polish recitation of the complete rosary. In said Rosary is found the conception, the birth, the youthful years, the sweat and tears in life, and then the death, but still the devotion of the Poles to the mystery of the Blessed Mother, even with their practical proverbs.

A ROBUST AND ENTERPRISING HOMESTEADER

Born in 1835 in Poland. With her forester husband they settled in Coldwater, Michigan, during the Civil War. Husband killed in timber accident in 1866. Subsequently married a widower. They then homesteaded in Section 9, Posen Township, Michigan, in 1870, paying $14.00 for 160 acres of virgin land.

Frances (nee Pawlak) Wojtych Scheminsky (Szymanski) was the village correspondent. She corresponded in both the Polish and German language.

Picture taken in 1916. Frances died in 1920, age 85.

THE RUGGED HOMESTEADER'S CABIN

THE CABIN WITH THE CHIMNEY

The sixteen by twenty-four foot homesteader's lob cabin was constructed in 1870. It then had a shingle roof, one door and two windows.

THE NOTCHED ENDS OF THE LOGS

Note the notched ends of the logs of this log cabin. The Polish homesteaders were foresters and wood-workers, originally from the Poznan and Pomerania Provinces. The skill in construction of this cabin has withstood all of the elements for over a hundred years, including the danger of fires and lightning.

THE FORESTER-HOMESTEADER'S BARN

Picture one

This twenty by twenty-eight foot barn was built in 1870 (National Archive Records). In constant use since that year, the barn is located in Section 9, Posen, Michigan.

Picture two

This notching of logs for the barn was another style of construction. Such notching has also withstood the elements for over a century. This barn and the cabin should have a historical marker to honor these homesteaders.

36
PRESQUE ISLE POLES

After Presque Isle County received its own entity, the first census commenced on August 13, 1870.

It listed the township of Rogers City, county of Presque Isle, having its post office at Alpena, Michigan, and the census enumerator was an assistant marshall named Benouin Lachance. On the first page it listed a Frederick Barnum, age 48, having real estate property in the value of $10,000 and having eight children.

In the vicinity of Grand Lake was a John Kaufman, he then being 37 years of age, born in Wurtenburg, residing with his wife Elizabeth and four sons. Also in the Grand Lake area was the lighthouse keeper Patrick Garrighty, age 45, born in Ireland, residing with his wife Mary and they having five children.

At that time the county of Presque Isle was in subdivision 12, the Eastern District of Michigan, as enumerated in 1870 according to the National Archives records.

The man who could be considered the founder of Rogers City and Presque Isle County was listed in the census as Albert Molitor, age 29. It stated that he was a lumber man born in Wurtenburg, having real estate property in the value of $63,000. He resided with his wife Lucille, age 24, and their son Albert, age 2. It should be noted that Molitor was shot in Rogers City in 1875, actually by the men who came up there to work for him, and many of them after working for him obtained homesteads. In fact, the one who paid the most for the crime by serving a prison term received a homestead there in 1872. Molitor is dealt with in other parts of the book.

Some of the people of Polish extraction that were counted in the census of 1870 were in fact the same people enumerated in Bronson, Michigan, Branch County, in the census of 1870. One of the Poles was a Michael Doias (Dojas) who was 47 years of age, and he is considered one of the early homesteaders. It should be noted that his son Joseph, age 8, was born in 1862 in Indiana.

Other Poles listed at that time were Lawrence Kowalski, with his wife Anna and four children; Valentine Lassenski (Losinski), with his wife and their three children, John, Joseph, and Josephine; and a Lawrence Przesbela (Przybyla). A homesteader by the name of Jacob Swaller, he then being 25 years of age and a native of Prussia, was listed as a farmer having a real estate in the value of $300.00.

There are also other Poles listed in the census of 1870; however, some of the earlier Poles, that is months ahead of the ones listed, were not listed in this census report. This is possibly due to the assistant marshall not being familiar with the area and could not find the so-called "cabin in the woods" of the homesteaders.

On page 7, line 21, dwelling 57, which was a hotel, it listed a Theadesea D. Larke, age 27. The enumerator did not have the correct first, or Christian, name because it should have been Frederick. This Larke was listed as a physician and surgeon and resided in the hotel. Mr. Larke eventually became the County Clerk and in the opinion of the writer you could call Mr. Larke "Mr. Presque Isle" due to his understanding that was shown to all the homesteaders and the farmers.

It should be noted that there are other persons listed in the census whose names correspond to the names of those obtaining land according to the land records in Maryland of the National Archives.

After August 20, 1870, the assistant marshall left Presque Isle County. Little did he realize that that fall or the winter of 1870-71 these rugged individuals in Presque Isle County witnessed a very severe winter. There were extreme temperatures, a great amount of snow, a very late spring, and, as dealt with in other books and articles, they almost perished due to lack of food in this, the then rugged part of Michigan with its beautiful virgin forests.

[POLISH "PERKI"!]

37
POLES ORGANIZE PRESQUE ISLE

"The first annual township meeting thereof shall be held at the dwelling of Lawrence Kowolsky (Kowalski) in said Presque Isle Township on the 16th day of August, 1871, at 10 o'clock in the forenoon. And at said meeting, three electors of said township shall be the persons whose duty it shall be to preside at such meeting, appoint a clerk, open and keep the polls, and exercise the same powers as the inspectors of elections at any township meeting as the law provides." These are the minutes of the meeting which was held at the Office of County Clerk, Alpena County, Michigan, on July 29, 1871. (Bentley Historical Library, Ann Arbor).

A resolution was brought before the township board on July 7, 1871, and this resolution was adjourned until July 29, 1871.

The record further indicates that the Alpena Board of Supervisors held their meeting at the Office of the County Clerk on the 29th day of July, 1871, at 2:00 P.M. The meeting was immediately called to order by the chairman.

A supervisor of Alpena County, Albert Molitor, presented the following information which was adopted by all the supervisors voting in the affirmative, in the matter of the application of nineteen persons from Presque Isle County, among them being William Rzepa, August Kowalski, Julius Paul, Michael Dojas, plus three other persons of Polish extraction.

The application was for the erection and organization of

a new township–it appearing to the Board of Supervisors that such application has been made and the notice thereof has been signed.

This record of the supervisors meeting further stated that "Posted up and published as in the manner required by law, and having duly considered the matter of said application, the Board orders and enacts that the territory described in said application bounded as follows, to wit: Towns No. 33 North, Range 5, 6, 7, 8 and 9 East, all in the County of Presque Isle in the State of Michigan, and Towns No. 34 North, Range 6, 7, and 8 East, in said County and State be and the same is hereby erected into a township to be called and known as the Township of Presque Isle. It should be noted that in that time of history Presque Isle County was under the jurisdiction of Alpena County.

The reason that the three other supervisors of said Alpena County agreed to such separate partition into Presque Isle County was that Supervisor Molitor who had the northern jurisdiction wanted to rule such jurisdiction by himself.

The first meeting mentioned was at the homestead of Lawrence Kowalski who could be termed the stalwart of the then area of Presque Isle County.

Kowalski's homestead was in Section 3 of the present Posen Township which section is presently alongside of M-65, north and across the road from the Polish cemetery in Posen, Michigan.

With the numerous Poles who wanted to earn their independence which was gained for all of Presque Isle County, it should be noted that the Poles in Posen and present Pulaski Township in 1875 wanted to be annexed by Alpena County due to the tactics of Albert Molitor.

38
DIVORCED 1872–MURDERED 1875

At the Bentley Historical Library, Ann Arbor, Michigan, it lists the chancery records of Presque Isle County, Michigan, and the first case in Liber 1, page 1, dealt with a divorce. This is written because the defendant in this equity suit was one of the first pioneers of Presque Isle County who encouraged the Poznanians, Pomeranians, Kashubians, and the Prussians to obtain employment and/or homesteads in Presque Isle County.

The Judgment of Divorce Decree stated:

STATE OF MICHIGAN
THE CIRCUIT COURT FOR THE
COUNTY OF PRESQUE ISLE–IN CHANCERY

Lucille Moliter, Complainant
vs.
Albert Moliter, Defendant

> At a session of said Court held at the Court House in the Village of Rogers City, in said County, on the eighth day of August, in the year one thousand and eight hundred and seventy two.
>
> Present: HONORABLE SANFORD M. GREEN,
> CIRCUIT JUDGE

THIS CAUSE having been brought on to be heard upon the Bill of Complaint, answer and proofs, and upon the report of Clinton Davidson, Commissioner of said Court, to whom it was referred by an order heretofore entered therein to take proofs of the material facts charged in such Bill of Complaint and report the same to said Court with his opinion thereon:

On reading the Bill of Complaint report of such Commissioner on the proofs accompanying the same from which it satisfactorily appeared to this Court that the material facts charged in such Bill of Complaint are true and that the defendant Albert Moliter had been guilty of the several acts of extreme cruelty therein charged and that said defendant is an unsuitable person to have the care, custody and maintenance of a minor child.

Albert Moliter the issue of their said marriage and named in said Bill and that the Complainant Lucille Moliter is a suitable person to have the care, custody and maintenance of said Child.

ON MOTION, J. B. Tuttle of counsel for said complainant,

IT IS ORDERED, ADJUDGED, AND DECREED, and this Court by virtue of the authority therein vested and in pursuance of the Statute in such case made the provided,

DOTH ORDER, ADJUDGE, AND DECREE, that the marriage between the said complainant Lucille Moliter and said defendant Albert Moliter is to be dissolved and the same is hereby dissolved accordingly and a divorce from the bonds of matrimony between said parties is also adjudged and decreed.

AND IT IS ALSO FURTHER ORDERED, ADJUDGED AND DECREED, that said complainant Lucille Moliter have the care, custody, and maintenance of said minor child, Albert Moliter, and that said child shall remain with said complainant Lucille Moliter until he shall attain the age of twenty-one years or until the further Order of the Court.

Sanford M. Green
Circuit Judge
Fred' Denny Larke, Register

Molitor (Moliter is in error in spelling in the case) did not have to pay child support. The divorce of today is similar to the divorce of 1872, the only exceptions being that a child is considered an adult when he is eighteen years of age; no fault of either party, eliminating perjury; but support of children is in a quandry.

From all the recorded history and information handed down from generation to generation, it is known that the defendant, Albert Molitor, had a hobby of being entertained by more than one woman. This entertaining of other and numerous women by Molitor lasted three years after the divorce. Molitor's hobby came to an end when he was shot in Rogers City, Michigan, by his own employees in August of 1875. Taken by lake ship to Detroit for hospitalization, he died in Detroit in September 1875.

When the news reached Presque Isle County that Albert Molitor died from the wound, the residents declared it a holiday, stating: "It could have never happened to a better guy." This in essence had the meaning that Molitor's ruthless way of handling the homesteaders and his employees will never again be witnessed by the inhabitants of the now peaceful county, as the "LORD AND RULER" received homesteaders' Justice.

39
NO DICTATOR IN MICHIGAN

The Poles who came to Michigan wanted no part of Prussian oppression because the Prussians took the land and forest away from them and compelled each Pole to serve approximately four years in the Prussian Army.

Upon arriving in Michigan they easily obtained employment because they knew the lumbering business as they were foresters and worked in woodshops in the area of Pomerania and Poznan. Many of them settled around the area of Hillsdale and Coldwater, Michigan, and eventually had their own community called Bronson, Michigan.

In 1870 a Jesuit priest by the name of Francis Xavier Schulak arrived in Bronson, Michigan, and informed the people that a secular priest Reverend Joseph Molitor, had a relative who was a lumber baron in northeastern Michigan, namely, Presque Isle County.

Many of the Poles from Branch County, Michigan, along with the Poles from St. Joseph County, Indiana, took the train to Detroit, Michigan, where at the Land Grant Office they paid $14 for 160 acres of land.

These foresters worked in the lumber mills and at the same time homesteaded their land, hence they were foresters and farmers.

These Poles, who were educated in Poland and knew the German and English languages, immediately set up Posen Township. They appointed and/or elected their officials and, of course, the supervisor of any township sat on the County Board.

In 1875 it became unbearable to listen to the dictator of northeastern Michigan whose domain was all of Presque Isle County. This Albert Molitor controlled every phase of a person's life.

Molitor tried to control all of the politics; in fact, one of the reasons Presque Isle County was given its own entity was because the people in Alpena County would not have anything to do with Albert Molitor.

In the summer of 1875, the Polish people, who knew the oppression they received in Prussian Poland, wanted to be ruled by themselves as they were hard workers and very rugged.

The Bentley Historical Library at Ann Arbor reveals that on July 10, 1875, most of the Polish officials from the Township of Posen went to the meeting in Rogers City and wanted Posen to leave the county jurisdiction.

Of course, they were turned down. But the Poles maintained that they were just as close to Alpena and Alpena had a port where many vessels and ships arrived, thereby having a market for their farm products and lumber.

With the foresight of these Poles in 1875, they never again submitted a request of seceding from Presque Isle County because in August of 1875 Albert Molitor was shot and the following month he died in Detroit, Michigan.

So the old saying that they who rule themselves, rule the best, was even applicable over one hundred years ago.

40
SWAMP "GOLD" DOWSERS

Water in an abundant supply was a basic requirement for any nascent community throughout recorded history, and Michigan was no exception.

When the Michigan forests were timbered, the early settlers purchased such land for the purpose of farming.

Many foresters with families purchased the cut-over timber land, prior to the Civil War. The main factor prior to purchasing such land was to hire a waterfinder. He was to determine a spot where the artesian well could be found.

Veins of water had to be found before a well was dug. Such a well had to be dug with a shovel, as during that time of history there were no well-drilling rigs.

It is alleged that the forked stick, used in locating water veins, originated in the area of Pomerania, Poland, and south of the Baltic Sea.

As the first Polish American foresters were from the Province of Pomerania, many *rozdzkarz* (waterfinders) were always in the migrating groups.

In the St. Joseph valley of Michigan and Indiana, there were two outstanding Polish Pomeranian waterfinders. They were always called *Pan* (Mister) Czorodzieski and *Pan* (Mister) Artezyjski. It was known that these two men, were "magicians" in determining where the artesian wells were found. Their locating water today would be considered dowsing.

The St. Joseph valley Polish American foresters arrived in 1869 and 1870 in Northeastern Michigan for employment.

These Poles decided to obtain a homestead in Presque

Isle County, Michigan. In 1870 this land was all virgin forest, and the cost of the land was $14.00 for 160 acres. On Sundays they evaluated the available homestead lands, then to the Detroit Land Office, where a homestead application was filed.

Knowing the areas of the particular sections, the foresters being knowledgeable in water-finding, they made excellent selections of their homestead lands.

Pan Czorodzielski would always determine the location of the water veins, maintaining that the secret of choosing wood for the special forked stick has been in the family since the 14th century. Czorodzielski's ability for locating water veins was in the class of a genious. (However, he could not determine how deep the well was to be dug before striking water).

Whether Czorodzielski could or could not determine the depth was never fully revealed. Some homesteaders maintained that the travelling water finders were *Szwagiers* (brother-in-laws) and worked as a team, hence, double income due to the dual ability and dual charges.

After Czorodzielski found the water veins, Mr. Artezyjski would charge a quarter eagle gold coin to disclose the depth where water would be found. Then the well was dug, usually 12 feet. (Well depth determined from the National Archives Land Records, Washington, D.C.).

The *szwagier* team always worked as a team. In the evening they would entertain the homesteader's children with magical tricks. This would be performed if the homesteader's supper consisted of beans, beef, ham, potatoes, corn in season, and of course cognac, and such entertainment was for the free supper.

On Sunday, the *szwagiers'* would entertain and sell "medicine" water, from a secret well deep in the virgin forests. This secret well story was always told at Polish social gatherings, in a version of the "Polish fountain of youth."

The homesteaders knew that a road would be built. The due north and due south road, between Sections 33 and 34, then south between Sections 28 and 27, then south between Section 4 and 3, 10 and 9, and 16 and 15. This road is the present M-65, running through the present village of Posen, Michigan, and into Pulaski Township.

In selecting the location for the well on the Northeast corner of Section 9, the "magical twins" *szwagiers* met the woman of the house. Frances' father was a forester, hence, her knowledge of selection of the well site was one that the "magical twins" held in amazement. It was presumed that Frances was the "Queen of the Dowsers."

Frances chose the well site, which was to be five chains and 25 links from the eastern line of section 9. This was 363 feet from the proposed road, close enough so man and beast could have water when the road would be built and completed. She was a gregarious person in temperament, and spoke to everyone.

The women and/or children always filled the wooden buckets in the artesian wells, and poured the water into a hollowed-out pine log. Thus, the passing oxen teams (later horses) always had sufficient water.

Any person in travel would stop by this sweet water well. Lowering the wooden bucket and removing the hanging ladle, passersby would consume the water to eliminate their thirst. Any water-holding container would also be replenished from this well by the travellers.

The *szwagiers* located and dug many wells in four townships, Posen, Pulaski, Krakow, and Metz. Some farms had three wells, if no stream passed through their sectioned lands for watering the grazing cattle and sheep, and irrigation in certain spots.

In 1876 the best land was all homesteaded. Everyone had sufficient wells. The "magical twins" then claimed that they could also detect minerals, so people could have their own salt mines, gravel pits, and possibly gold mines.

A speculating forester-farmer, not a homesteader, purchased low land from the State. Such land was not arable agricultural land, but only pasture land, and near a swamp.

The speculator, Mr. Ryzykant, claimed on certain dark nights there was a sparkling reflection on his low land, an indication of valuable minerals underneath such land. Ryzykant wrote a letter to the "magical twins" informing them that if they detected minerals and dug for such minerals, Ryzykant would split such quick profits, 50%-50%. If these *szwagiers* can find water, they can find gold was deduced by the speculator, and so informed the *szwagiers*.

The *szwagiers*, known opportunists, visited the low land of Mr. Ryzykant. Having "advanced" instruments by then, and after being paid for their initial investigation and research, the "magical twins" made a final conclusion and report.

They informed the speculator that his property had "swamp gas," but science was not far enough advanced to profitably mine such valuable "swamp gas."

Incidently, the sweet water wells dug in 1870 are still providing fresh water. The writer tasted this water again in 1976 when visiting Section 9.

The secret "medicine" water well, the "Polish fountain of youth," was never found, but the story continues to date.

The low land is presently pasture land where the sparkling reflection of the "swamp gas" is not gold, but beef cattle prior to being shipped to the slaughter house.

41
LIBRARIES AND GOOD BOOKS

Just south of the 50th parallel, that is 50 degrees north, is the village and farming community of Netcie, Czechoslovakia.

Netcice is 125 miles east southeast of Prague, Czechoslovakia, and 125 miles west southwest of Krakow, Poland.

Records at the *Statni Archiv* at *Brno*, Czechoslovakia, reveal that on June 20, 1809, Ignatius Shulak, twenty years of age, of Netcice, was married to Anna Bayer, age 23. The couple settled in the town of Netcice.

Every day for sixteen years the couple prayed in order that God would give them a child.

Shortly before Christmas in House No. 30, in the Village of Netcice, there was joy because on December 17, 1825, the couple were the proud parents of a boy they named Francis. Francis grew up in this little village and helped his father to work the farm. Francis received his education from his parents and the village priest.

This village was in the Moravia district which was then in the Austrian kingdom.

On September 13, 1845, Francis entered the Society of Jesus in Krakow, Poland.

After finishing his basic studies he was appointed prefect and a teacher at the school of natural science for ten years at a Jesuit high school and college in Tarnopol, Poland.

At the college he began to organize a botanological department. This department was later transferred to Chyrow, Poland.

Father Shulak had furthered his education at Poznan, Poland; then at the Paris Bibliography (the largest library of studies in Paris, France); and then he studied the English language in London, England.

He departed from Liverpool, England, and arrived in New York in the year 1865 and was sent to the Jesuit province in Missouri where he continued his English studies and also served as a missionary to the Polish, Czech, and the non-Polish settlements in and around the area of St. Louis, Missouri.

The Archives from the province in Krakow, Poland, stated that his main duty was to educate the immigrants through the establishment of parish libraries and by encouragement to read good books and to form youth organizations.

The Messenger of the Sacred Heart Magazine was sent from Krakow at the request of Father Shulak.

As a liberal in that time of History Father Shulak paid no attention to any criticism, difficulties and other road blocks in his trying to set the needs of the people. Father Shulak stated that preaching alone is inefficient in fortifying the Bible, but that in addition to the Bible other good publications were needed. With that in mind Father Shulak planned and established many libraries. Upon establishing such libraries he introduced something in the Middle West which hereto before had not existed.

Father Shulak's main contention was to battle ignorance and illiteracy. After establishing a few libraries in Missouri, which he called "the library of the good book," he ran into conflict with his superiors and in 1869 he was transferred to Chicago, Illinois.

In Illinois he immediately commenced travelling and sailing to establish posts to dispense information and ideas.

Father Shulak did not fall in spirit due to the unfair judgments that were made of him. He continued to travel in all areas of the Great Lakes holding Forty Hours Devotion, preaching at missions, holding novenas, and travelling to established lumber camps. In his travel to Indiana and Branch County, Michigan, he informed the Poles who worked as foresters in Branch County, Michigan, and as woodworkers in the Indiana area that there was land in northeastern Michigan that could be homesteaded.

The Poles of Branch County, Michigan, and St. Joseph County, Indiana, who began arriving in the Middle West in 1858, took the advice of Father Shulak and purchased such homesteads in Presque Isle County. Numerous others went to Alpena County in Michigan.

Father Shulak established St. Casimir's in Posen, named St. Ignatius Church in Rogers City after his father, and gave many missions in Alpena, Bay City, Cheboygan, Saginaw, Port Huron, and other ports as he sailed the Great Lakes in the role as a spiritual adviser.

Manuscripts obtained from the Archives in Krakow, Poland, indicate That Father Shulak prepared to return to Poland for his retirement in August of 1906. He then visited Posen and Alpena, Michigan, being 81 years of age.

From Alpena he travelled to Detroit, Michigan, then to Guelph, Ontario, where he said mass for his classmate, Father Gaspar Matoga, S.J.. He then returned to Detroit, from Detroit to New York, where he sailed to France and in France he said mass at Lourdes.

He then returned to Krakow, Poland, where he had been educated, and on January 19, 1908, Father Shulak died.

Father Shulak labored in the United States as a missionary for forty-three years and was a member of the Society of Jesus for sixty-three years.

The Poles in northeastern Michigan settled there because of the foresight of Father Shulak. At the libraries and archives at the University of Michigan and the University of Notre Dame, numerous PH. D. dissertations mention Father

Shulak being in various parts in the Great Lakes area. With the work done by this saintly priest, it would be a tribute if some group in any of the communities he served would either erect a statue in his honor or otherwise commence action for his canonization. In one instance, his sailing vessel landed at False Presque Isle, Michigan, and Father Shulak with his vestments, chalice, etc., walked fifteen miles to his homesteaders through the dense virgin forests, not level roads as today, to offer mass in a homesteaders log cabin, he then being fifty years of age. This alone is sufficient cause for beatification, in my humble opinion. NOTE: The surname Shulak was used in this article, as in June, 1874.

Father Shulak purchased land in N.E. Michigan under such surname. The real name is Schulak, but it was also spelled Szulak. The records in the Czechoslovakia Archives, and the Archives in Krakow, Poland use the name Schulak.

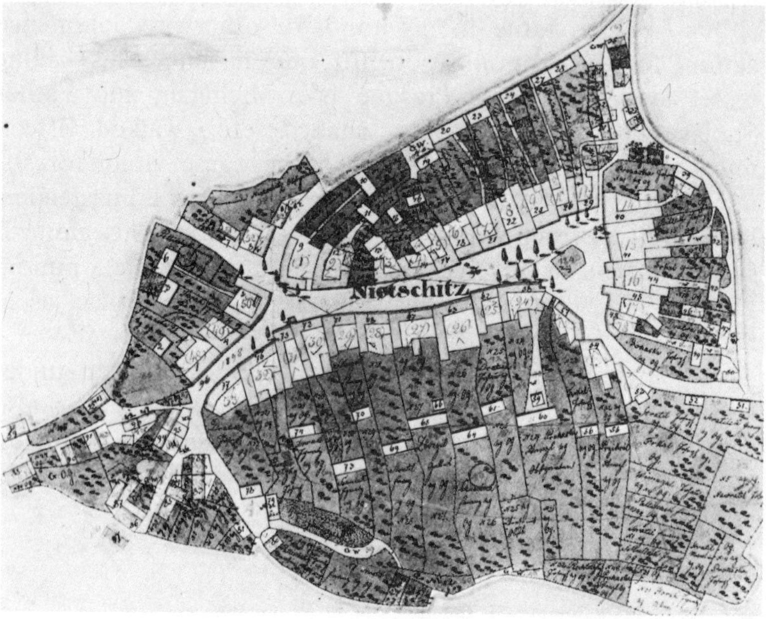

THE BIRTHPLACE OF THE "SAINTLY" SAILING MISSIONARY

BIRTHPLACE OF REV. FRANCIS X. SCHULAK, S.J. NETCICE, PRESENTLY IN CZECKOSLOVAKIA.

BORN on December 17, 1825, in House #30, section 72. His great-grandfather was born here on March 29, 1713. From the records at Statni Archiv, Brno.

42
MADMAN MOLITOR

Albert Molitor, an opportunist all of his life, is responsible for attracting the Poles and Germans to Presque Isle County. The reason Molitor brought the Poles and Germans was because he knew that they were hard workers.

In all of the records of the National Archives and other books that have been read about Albert Molitor, it can be stated that he would say anything to please anyone. He was obsessed with attaining great power and wealth.

Molitor stated that his mother was "Madame Franciska von Molitor"; however, the records indicate that she was only a serving maid.

The military records of the National Archives indicate that Molitor enrolled with the Union Army on December 20, 1861, for a period of three years, he then being 28 years of age.

He received an appointment as First Lieutenant with the 13th Independent Battery, the New York Light Artillery.

What he did in the first nine months of service is not known. At the Headquarters of the First Corps, the Army of Virginia, at Mary Hall's Farm, on the 9th of September, 1862, a surgeon by the name of J. Cantwell who stayed at Hall's Farm, wrote a letter stating:

"1st Lt. Albert Molitor, detailed to Maj. General J. Sigel's staff, having applied for a certificate on which to ground an application for leave of absence, I do hereby certify that I have carefully examined this officer, and find that he is suffering from prungo and chronic diarrhea.

"And that, in consequence thereof, he is, in my opinion, unfit for duty. I further declare my belief that he will not be able to resume his duties in a less period than fifteen days."

This was a very smart maneuver by Molitor because on the same day he wrote a letter to Major General J. Sigel, Commander, First Corps of the Army. In the letter Molitor stated:

"General!

Respectfully referring to the within testimony of Surg. Cantwell, I request you will grant a leave of absence for fifteen days to Washington to the undersigned.

Very respectfully
Yours most obedient Servt.

Albert Molitor
1st Lt. detailed to the Staff
of the 1st Corps of the Armie."

The reason for Molitor's maneuvering is that the Central Guard House in Washington, D.C., on September 20, 1862, ordered "arrest Lieutenant Molitor for stealing a U.S. horse." This was addressed to the Commander of the Central Guard House.

Subsequent writings by Molitor were dated in Washington, D.C., on November 21, 1862, wherein he wrote a letter to Major General Sigel, Commander of the Reserve Corps of the Army of the Potomac. He stated: "The undersigned most respectfully begs leave to tender *unconditionally* and *immediately* his resignation as 1st Lieutenant of the 13th Battery, New York Light Voluntary Infantry. The reason that prompted him to take this step is to be found in the malicious dealings of his Captain, Cpt. Julius Dieckmann, towards him, as officially proven by General Orders No. 38, wherein is said: 'And the Court did therefore honorably acquit the accused, First Lieut. Albert Molitor, 13th Battery, N.Y.V. Art., and find that the prosecution seems to have been prompted by malice.' " It was signed "Very respectfully, Your most obedient servant, Albert Molitor, First Lieutenant, 13th Battery, detailed to the staff of the 11th Corps.

In Washington, on November 21, 1862, after Albert Molitor tendered his resignation, he asked for a leave of absence until his resignation was accepted, the reason: he being dissatisfied.

On November 23, 1862, this resignation was referred to Captain Schirmer, who was the Chief of Artillery and Ordnance, and was referred by order of Major General Sigel. On November 25, 1862, Captain Schirmer, Chief of the Artillery, received a letter stating: "Within application for resignation respectfully recommended, and leave of absence granted until said resignation be accepted." It was signed by the Commander of the 13th New York Battery, being Captain Julius Dieckmann. On November 28, 1862, that recommendation was submitted to Major General J. Sigel for further consideration by the Commanding Officer of the Chief of the Artillery of the 11th Corps. This letter was respectfully returned for the opinion of Captain Schirmer, Chief of Artillery and Ordnance, by order of Major General Sigel.

On November 29, 1862, at Headquarters of the 11th Corps, it stated: "Respectfully returned with the opinion that Lieutenant Molitor has no good reason for tendering his resignation. That the military law will protect him against any malice from Captain J. Dieckmann. I therefore disapprove his resignation and recommend that he be ordered back immediately to his Battery for duty." It was again signed by Captain Schirmer.

However, on December 8, 1862, Headquarters of the 11th Corps, the Army of the Potomac, at Fairfax, ordered honorable discharge. It was signed and approved by the Adjutant General.

Another record reveals that there was an Officers Casualty List where it stated that on November 8, 1862, (wherein actually it should be December 8, 1862), A. Molitor received his discharge–casualty being Resd., which would stand for resigned.

Other military records in the National Archives revealed that in February 1862 Molitor was absent in arrest awaiting a general court martial. In April 1862 he was absent–sick in Washington–but the records indicated that he received an honorable discharge under a special order on December 8, 1862, which reveals basic dishonesty.

It should be noted that part of the records in the National Archives were expunged on January 7, 1891, no reason being given.

With all the maneuvering, chicanery, and tricks that Molitor played, he met his last trick in the year of 1875 when he was shot by some of his disgruntled workers in Rogers City, Michigan. In all the articles read and researched, Molitor never gave the same two answers. It can be stated that Molitor played his tricks once too often and such tricks were not accepted by the homesteaders, especially when he controlled the whole County of Presque Isle.

There is much more to be written about Molitor, but it can be said that he was the first mad man in northeastern Michigan–a mad man among the peaceful pines and peaceful Poles. But he was shot, not by a Pole, but by one of his own men from his own country.

43
CHOLERA CURTAINS PASSENGER PIGEONS

Cholera is an Asiatic word and an Asiatic ailment that has afflicted humans, birds, and animals. When cholera spread through Europe it even reached the northern part of Poland up to and including the Baltic Sea area. This word, "cholera", is a polite modified version of a cuss word among the Poles.

The reason this ailment is mentioned is because in an affidavit in a National Archive it was revealed that then the Polish foresters arrived in Detroit in 1854, cholera was very prevalent and many such Poles and their children lost their lives.

Furthermore, there are many versions of cholera and it is this writer's theory that a strain of this cholera was the reason for the extinction of the passenger pigeon.

Autumn brought the huge flocks of the migrating passenger pigeons to the southwestern part of Michigan, especially to the St. Joseph Valley which extended into Indiana.

The residents in that area informed the newly arrived Poles of the migration and that passenger pigeons were overabundant, and these birds almost killed each other in flight. These passenger pigeons were a delicacy and everyone used them for provisions.

During the Civil War era the Michigan Poles when first observing and inspecting these passenger pigeons compared them to the prolific turtledoves that were in the peaceful forest and meadows of Pomerania and Poznan Provinces. Such turtledoves served as food in the ecological cycle.

Having constantly been admonished in the Old Country not to waste food, the Michigan Poles accepted the surplus pigeons given them by their non-Polish neighbors. In Poland they smoked the breasts of these matured pigeons for winter use, and the young pigeons were used for squab soup.

The wings, backs, thighs and drumsticks were made into a potted passenger pigeon dish which today is called a casserole.

The heart and innards were fed to the barnyard cats. The surplus was smoke dried for the winter supply, to be fed to the watch-work dogs and, of course, the cats.

Nothing was wasted in that era of history as every winter the supply of food required preparation and storage.

When these Poles homesteaded to northeastern Michigan in 1870 they were amazed at the number of the nesting passenger pigeons especially in the beech trees. The beech-nut trees were along the rivers, streams, and the bays. The residents in that part of Michigan *did not* hunt these pigeons for commercial purposes as adequate transportation did not exist. The people in that part of Michigan ate and preserved the birds; they never sold them, as there was no railroad until 1886. Furthermore, this area of Michigan would be in isolation during the winter months, hence provisions were stored for an adequate supply of food for themselves.

This recipe, which was brought from Poland, was applied to the passenger pigeon, in the preparation for an evening meal. The recipe is:

Eight passenger pigeons
Two cups of flour
One tablespoon of sour salt (coarse)
½ teaspoon pepper (if available)

The milk and eggs were added to the above ingredients and the meat was coated evenly.

These were usually sauteed in butter, however from 1870 to 1875 it could have been lard, goose grease, or bacon drippings.

Sauté the birds in the butter for about six minutes. Then pour two cups of boiling water over the birds. Cover the pot tightly. Roast for about one hour at 325 degrees. Keep the pot moist by adding water. The last thirty minutes add fresh mushrooms and then a gravy can be made. These were eaten with rice or potatoes.

In the area of northeastern Michigan there were many beech, maple and oak trees. The oak trees produced acorns and, of course, the beech trees produced beechnuts, which the passenger pigeons consumed in great quantity.

It should be noted that in this area of Michigan the beech trees and limestones were in abundance and these two were compatible to the passenger pigeons as there was a sufficient amount of fine stones and fine gravel which the birds used as grit.

As stated previously the nests of these passenger pigeons were similar to the turtledove nests in Poland. Such nests are comparable to the mourning doves presently in Michigan, however the mourning doves have two eggs to a nest where usually passenger pigeons had one.

Their droppings were fertilizer and, of course, this made the oak and beech trees grow to proportionate heights.

In that part of Michigan the skies would be darkened as they always flew in groups.

Many of the young squabs were used for soup and this was used as a medicine, which pacified infants when they were afflicted with the common children's ailments.

It is stated that during migration when these birds flew along the western part of Lake Huron they would fly into the masts of the sailing ships and many Great Lakes seamen had this delicacy–roasted or broiled passenger pigeon.

In 1875 the Michigan Legislature passed an act imposing a penalty for maiming pigeons near nestings.

In essence, the law, which was approved on April 23, 1875, provided for the penalty for maiming pigeons near nestings and was so amended:

"Sec. 9. No person or persons shall use any gun or guns, or fire-arms, to maim, kill, or destroy any wild pigeon or pigeons, at or within five miles of the place or places where they are gathered in bodies for the purpose of breeding their young, known as pigeon nestings; and no person or persons shall use any gun or guns, or fire-arms, to maim, kill, or destroy any wild pigeon or pigeons within their roostings anywhere within the limits of this State; and no person or persons shall, with trap, snare, or net, or in any other manner, take or attempt to take, or kill or destroy, or attempt to kill or destroy, any wild pigeon (or pigeons), at or within two miles of such nesting place at any time from the beginning of the nesting until after the last hatching of such nesting, anywhere within the limits of this State: and every person offending against the provisions of this section, or any part thereof, shall be subject to a penalty of fifty dollars, with costs of suit."

The people of northeastern Michigan used an old Polish proverb: "*Zbytek kazi pozytek*", which translated and in essence means: "Luxury contaminates the common advantage."

During 1875 a travelling Polish attorney, one *Advokat* Ranyc, who was educated in an Eastern school, would travel to the various Polish settlements and communities and he informed the people in northeastern Michigan that the law makers in Lansing passed the statute, thereby nobody would be bothering the passenger pigeon's nests in the virgin forests of hardwood, mainly oak and beech.

Advokat Ranyc stated that the horn of plenty or the cornucopia (in Polish it is *rog obfitosci*) would not last. This Ranyc also used the Polish proverb of "*Zyc, nie umierac!*" which means "live, not die!" (or "This is the life!").

Ranyc enjoyed such Polish squab dinners and as he stated these squabs were to be consumed only in moderation and only for festivities.

The Polish forester farmers warned the people about the declining nesting grounds of the passenger pigeons. They knew that the forests in Poland were preserved for centuries for the perpetuation of the beast and fowl.

The absentee lumber barons ignored such ecological warnings and they kept stripping the forests. However the forester-farmers did not cut down their virgin beech and oak trees as the dead limbs and the thinnings of these forests provided for their fuel and heat.

There were many theories regarding the passenger pigeons–of their slaughter, their killing, and their dense roosts. However, the Polish forester farmers detected that the passenger pigeons were afflicted with some type of disease. From past experience in Poland they knew that if a certain bird was afflicted then it would be many years before such species of bird would make its comeback.

In 1901 the Michigan Legistlature passed Public Act 217 wherein they stated that no person shall kill, capture, or destroy or attempt to kill, caputre, or destroy by any means whatever, any dove or homing pigeon within the limits of the state. It further stated, "or any wild pigeon until the year nineteen hundred ten, and then only at the time, in the manner, and for the purpose authorized by law."

This was too late for the passenger pigeon for passing such a Public Act as it was the disease of cholera that led the passenger pigeon to extinction. It was repeated many times that there were passenger pigeons in Presque Isle County, Michigan, in the year 1903.

The writer vividly recollects the stories of the passenger pigeons as were told to him by his grandfather who in turn received such stories from his cheerful mother-in-law who homesteaded in that area in 1870.

This was in the 1930's and these oldtimers witnessed the last of such passenger pigeon and it could be retold of the "Polish Prophecies" of the original homesteaders that these birds were inflicted with some type of ailments, hence the rapid diminishing of their flocks and eventual extinction.

THE POSEN, PULASKI, KRAKOW HIGHWAY

Digging, then shoveling the sand for the roadbed.

TOP PICTURE
The sand is hauled away. The team of horses are identical.
BOTTOM PICTURE
The road completed. This is M-65, Posen, Michigan. Looking north towards US-23, from the Posen Cemetery.

44
THE POSEN, PULASKI, KRAKOW HIGHWAY

The Pomerania Poles who arrived in Alpena and Presque Isle County in the year of 1870 in their homestead lands had to build highways. It should be noted that Pulaski Township was part of Posen Township in that era of history.

In the 1870's the Michigan Legislature enacted laws regarding stricter highway laws as to building of such highways. Each township had a Commissioner of Highways. He would assess the number of days to be worked in construction of such highways, basing it on the number of acres which was the real property evaluation and, of course, the general property. When the new law went into effect, it stated that the Commissioner of Highways shall have the general care and superintendence of highways therein, meaning within the township.

The roads at that time to be constructed are the present M-65, the Alpena Road, and East 3634, in addition to other roads. The Commissioner would then appoint an overseer in each road district. The overseer for each road district would see that all the highways were to be built and kept in repair, and such overseer shall cause the highway labor that was to be assessed.

If the landowner did not put in a day's work on the highway, he could pay one dollar. The landowner had to furnish a cart, wagon, a plow or scraper. Also required was a yoke of oxen and later a span of horses. A span at that time was a pair of animals, first mules, then horses, usually matched in looks and action and driven together. It was also required that a man had to manage the yoke of oxen or the span of horses.

For each day assessed each man had to work eight hours per day. The laws made provisions for loafers by stating that "after appearing, if remained idle, or not worked faithfully, or hindered others from working, such offender shall, for each offense, pay the sum of one dollar." Whether this was ever enforced is not known. However, highways were a necessity; hence, it is doubtful whether there were any loafers.

The overseer had the power to call out any persons in his district to remove obstructions from the highway, repair culverts or bridges that were injured by freshets or otherwise. A freshet at that time in history was a great rise or overflowing of a stream caused by heavy rain or melted snow.

The laws further stated that all road work done upon roads that have been open and worked for ten years or more, could become a permanent improvement of such roads by gravelling and turnpiking.

The improvements of such roads were elevations that could be cut down and depressions that could be raised to form a grade as level as the nature of the ground will permit.

The width of the turnpike shall not be less than ten feet on each side of the center line of the road.

Even then this maxim applied: "If you want something done, do it yourself." This maxim has reference to the new law which said any person shall be allowed to remove snow, to haul gravel or other material for the repair of the roads at any time during the year. It should be noted that in that era of history there were no men paid to plow the snow.

The law further stated that after the turnpike is used for

one year, that is, after the eleventh year, then (1) the ruts shall be filled; (2) the turnpike shall be gravelled (where gravel can be conveniently obtained). It continued by stating: In gravelling any road, the gravel shall be placed along the center, not less than eight feet in width, and in a mass, not less than six inches deep, or not to exceed fifteen inches. A lot of this work could be done after November 1 if the road bed was dry and in fit condition; hence, even a century ago some autumns were mild.

The Commissioner would establish the grade of such road, and he "shall set grade stakes not more than six rods (rod = 16½ feet) apart along the side of the highway to be worked."

In the first law under Section 15 it stated that "whenever the residents along any highway may wish to improve the same by paving or macadamizing, they may do so at their own expense and in such manner as may be approved by the Commissioner." Even then a person paying for self-improvement needed the permission of a bureaucrat, in this case, the Commissioner of Highways.

Also, the general duties of the Commissioner and overseer were: (1) cause the noxious weeds within limits of the highway to be cut down and destroyed twice a year, once before July and once before December (it should be noted at that time this cutting of weeds was done by hand with possibly a sickle); and (2) all the loose stones lying on the beaten track of the road to be removed.

It further stated that the overseer could procure a good and sufficient iron or steel-shod scraper and a suitable plow or either of them.

The Commissioner shall have the care of building, rebuilding, and repairing of all bridges where the cost exceeds $20. If the cost is over $50, the same shall be let by contract. The overseer had jurisdiction if the amount was under $20. The bridge repair, construction, etc., cannot exceed $1,000 a year for any one township.

The total usefulness of the ox in that era should be noted. When the ox was too old to work, it would be barbecued and served at weddings or other festivities.

It should be noted that if a mother-in-law had a $500 personal property value, such value would be assessed, and she had to work on the highway, that is at least one day. What she did was never recorded; hence, it is assumed that the son-in-law worked the extra day to have a good highway so the mother-in-law would visit other relatives. This is one of the reasons why the highways were constructed—so the mother-in-law would visit her other relatives. When the mother-in-law praised her son-in-law for completing his part of the highway, as he placed the mother-in-law on the sleigh for her to stay with other relatives, a Polish proverb would be appropriate. The proverb: *Nie ten majster kto zachal ale ten kto skonczyl.* This proverb translated means: He is not the master who started but he who finished.

Possibly this proverb, especially used in these three Polish townships, could be called Polish reciprocity, or "how to get along with a Polish mother-in-law."

45
SANDWICHES IN SHOE BOXES

In 1876 Michigan was still in a major depression. It was an election year so that various items that were to be exhibited at the Centennial celebration in Philadelphia were held to a minimum.

The round trip railroad fair from Detroit to Philadelphia was $23.40. Due to the competition and a shortage of spending money, in September of 1876 this fare was reduced to $18.

In the various villages and cities there were usually two newspapers. One was usually affiliated with the Republican Party and the other was affiliated with the Democratic Party. If there was a third newspaper in the county it was usually listed as an independent.

Various counties in their exhibits at the agricultural exhibits at Philadelphia sent samples. Macomb County sent the following samples:

Four-rowed barley
Wild goose spring wheat
Popcorn
Black-eyed marrow-fat peas
Lima, pole, purple wax and common field beans
Merino wool with the fleeces weighing from 7 to 29 lbs.
Yellow dent and calico corn
Mediterranean wheat

The variety of peaches grown in Michigan at that time were known as Early Ann, Early York, Morris White (the best flavored of any of the peaches is of this variety), Hill's Chili, and Barnard.

Apples at the Philadelphia exhibits from Michigan were the red russet, Porter, and also an improved Siberian crab. Later in the season the Crawford late peaches were in the exhibit.

Here at home in the State of Michigan the high school courses consisted of Caesar, Latin Prose, Botany, Physiology and also Intellectual Philosophy.

They had a State Reform School for Boys. In the Industrial Department the boys were taught to work in the shop and also on the farm. These boys attended school from 9 to 12 in the morning and they worked from 1 to 4 in the afternoon. The recorder of the events of the Centennial stated, "The other hours of the day have their appropriate allotments for the benefit of the students," that is, the students at the State Reform School.

On the university level at the universities they taught, of course, all policital economy which possibly would be a major in economics and another major in political science today.

At the University of Michigan, on April 16, 1876, Professor Watson, who was the Director of the Observatory and a Professor of Astronomy, discovered a planet.

At the Michigan State Agricultural College, presently known as Michigan State University, which was then an agricultural students' college, it was said that the students were employed and were paid ten cents an hour.

The unknown recorder stated "this labor is usually performed cheerfully and well." It should be noted that the State Board of Agriculture at that time had a member who was a resident of Romeo, Michigan, which is in Macomb County.

Another article of interest that should be noted was during that Centennial year the number of work oxen in Michigan was 38,901; ages not listed. The oxen were beasts of burden and after obtaining a certain age, they were used for ox roasts.

The capital invested in the wagon, carriage, and sleigh factories was $1,600,000, and it should be noticed that there were no cars in that period of history. What they produced in that year the value of the total products was $1,800,000, and of course nobody was subjected to income taxes.

Very few counties in Michigan during that depression year had an exhibit in Washington or at the State Fair Grounds then in the City of Detroit. However, the persons that submitted their samples in agricultural products received numerous honors in Philadelphia. These honors were brought back to Macomb County by the exhibitors, who on their journey from Philadelphia had the shoe boxes filled with dry sandwiches, the ribbons won, and, of course, the samples of their exhibits.

With the Centennial depression in 1876, and now the economic cycle at its nadir, most persons in Michigan would travel to Philadelhpia for the Bicentennial, if the round trip fare was $18.

Yes, at that price for the transportation, the Michigan residents would pack their own sandwiches in shoe boxes. However, today with the pre-packaged and pre-prepared foods, the train trip would be very enjoyable.

46
FIRST POLISH POSTMISTRESS

In the Industrial and Social Branch of the Civil Archives Division of the National Archives Records Service, it is revealed that the Post Office in Posen, Michigan, Presque Isle County, was established on February 24, 1875.

Frank Roshek was appointed the first postmaster on that date: however, he declined the position.

In the Centennial year on January 4, 1876, the postal records revealed that Mrs. Clara Jeziski (other spellings were Jezeski, but the correct spelling from the church records was Jezerski) was appointed postmaster.

Clara on her appointment was 57 years of age and resided with her husband Matthew Jezerski. Matthew born in Holland of Polish descent. The census records (1880) revealed that Clara could read and write, and it is listed that she was born in Prussia. Since Clara and her husband could both read and write, it can be assumed that they were educated in Europe.

Clara's husband, Matthew, was a farmer. Residing with Matthew and Clara was Clara's nephew, Frank Zabouski, age 23.

Due to an economy cut, the Posen Post Office was discontinued on January 16, 1877. For the next five years the people of the village of Posen received their mail out of Rogers City, Michigan.

Women's liberation existed in Poland long before the Centennial in the State of Michigan. Clara was a very intelligent woman who could speak German, Polish, Dutch and English fluently.

Everyone would smile when they went to the Post Office because they were not flooded with bills and junk mail. Postage cost two cents then.

It must have been a real pleasure to go to the Post Office on the red letter days when some good book or magazine came from Father Schulak. This Jesuit priest was advisor to the Polish people living in the Great Lakes area. His advice was practical as well as spiritual (*The Sailing Missionary* by NATSOLIM).

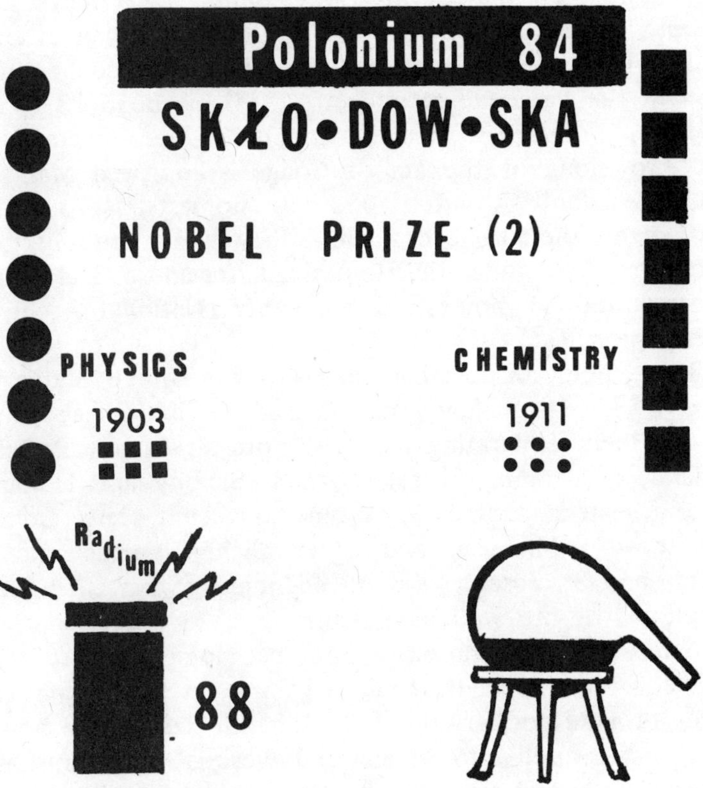

47

THE POSEN TOWNSHIP CENTENNIAL–1876

Michigan was in a depression in 1876 but the homesteading farmers of Posen Township, Presque Isle County, Michigan, knew that during the centennial year they "shall be entitled to a Patent for the Tract of Land" they entered and homesteaded. These rugged individuals made application at the Land Office at Detroit, Michigan, in 1870 and 1871. In order to receive the final certificate, pursuant "to the provisions of the act of Congress approved May 20, 1862, entitled 'An Act to secure homesteads to actual settlers on the public domain,'" they had to submit final proof required under the Homestead Act and a final affidavit required of homestead claimants (National Archives, Washington, D.C.).

These homesteaders had come to the United States between 1853-1865. Many had arrived as children accompanying their emigrating parents, foresters from Prussian Poland, Pomerania, Silesia, Poznan, Saxony and Holland. The foresters settled in Wayne, Oakland, and Branch Counties in Michigan and other Michigan areas, and in Noble and St. Joseph's Counties, Indiana, where they were employed by the Studebaker Company.

After the information about the Homestead Act was relayed, the applicants took a gamble in purchasing 160 acres of land for $14.00. With this application the homesteaders ventured into Alpena and Presque Isle County and entered upon and made "settlement on said land."

These homesteaders could read German and Polish, write Polish and Gothic German, and undoubtedly understood English, as they were educated in Europe and easily assimilated into the new virgin forest settlements in northeastern Michigan (1880 Census Records).

The community (township) Poles and Germans congregated from the eastern and southern sections at a place south of the present St. Casimer's Church. This property was purchased by Father Francis X. Schulak, S.J., in behalf of St. Ignatius College, Chicago, Illinois. The 40 acres was paid for in gold coins amounting to $100.00 on June 15, 1874 (*The Sailing Missionary* by NATSOLIM).

At about 4:00 a.m. on June 17, 1876, they began walking towards the other homesteaders in the northwestern sections who joined them for the trek to Rogers City, where they arrived shortly before 8:00 a.m. at the County Clerk's office.

In this trek were names as Reazek, Kowalski, Szymanski, Linke, Muszynski, Dojas, Strelecki, Loshinski, etc. A widow, Michaline Witucki (nee Pawlak), whose husband was killed felling trees on his homestead in 1871, also accompanied the group, along with her sister, Frances (nee Pawlak) Wojtych Szymanski, who was the village correspondent.

For the American Centennial in 1876, Frederick Larke, the Clerk of Presque Isle County, certified that "whose names are subscribed to the foregoing affidavit are persons of respectability" (Land Records, Maryland).

A Lorenz Kowalski and a Matthias Schemansky (Maciej Szymanski), on June 17, 1876, attested that Franz Reaszek (Frank Roshek), the first Polish settler, entered his land on June 28, 1870, and made it his exclusive home from the 16th of July, 1870. It was 124.6 acres and in Section 3 and 4, presently Highway 65 at Metz Highway, both sides of the highway. With his wife and one child, Roshek built a house 24′ X 16′, with one door, 3 windows, a board floor, a shingle roof; and a barn 36′ X 20′. Roshek departed from Posen about 1878, as his name is not listed in the 1879 church congregation list, or in the 1880 census. Roshek was from St. Joseph's County, Indiana, and his friend was Lorenz Kowalski, who finished his home on July 22, 1870.

Roshek and Szymanski attested that Lorenz Kowalski, "since said settlement, plowed, fenced and cultivated 15 acres of said land, and made the following imrovements thereon, to wit: 15 more (acres) chopped down, built a barn 30′ X 18′, dug a well 12′ deep, and planted 12 fruit trees," which orchards were in existence in 1930.

Kowalski also attested for John Christian Linke, who constructed the first two-story house in the area and had the best handwriting of all the homesteaders according to the records of the National Archives.

For $4.00, the successful homesteader had his 160 acres (or proportionate acreage) of land. According to National Archive records, the final certificate to the land (in essence a deed) was issued at the Detroit Land Office on June 18, 1876. What a beautiful gift for a centennial! All of the homesteaders by then were U.S. Citizens, so the great celebration that must have followed can only be imagined!

In 1870, the highest point in the county was selected as his 160-acre homestead by Matthias Schemansky (Maciej Szymanski), a widower with two sons, married to Frances Wojtych, nee Pawlak, a widow with two daughters. On October 24, 1870, they built a 20′ X 16′ shingle-roof, one-door, two-window home, and subsequently, a 20′ X 28′ barn, both buildings still in existence due to the durability of the timber selected and the knowledge of construction by the foresters. These two buildings were still in existence at the time of writing this article. The home of Frances' sister, Michaline (nee Pawlak) Witucki, built at about the same time, is still preserved. These buildings should be given historical markers. These two women, both married to foresters, lost their husbands in felling timber in that area.

The two stalwarts of the community, Lorenz Kowalski and Maciej Szymanski, along with Frank Roshek at times, signed all the affidavits of the homesteaders. Maciej, who was born in 1840, died in a timber accident on January 20, 1889, in Posen, Michigan, and is buried right in the cemetery and his tombstone can be seen from Highway M-65. Lorenz Kowalski, who also was born in 1840 (August 10th), died in Posen on December 2, 1917.

The two homesteaders, plus the personable Frank Roshek, encouraged other foresters, laborers, etc., to become homesteading farmers.

As the homesteaders arrived, the government applications became very complicated and asked "foolish" questions. The records in Maryland reveal that subsequent homesteaders built "a log shanty, temporarily erected, and about 2½ acres chopped, and 1½ acres cleaned up, and the value is $100.00" for the 160 acres, west of Posen.

The Homestead Pre-Exemption and Commutation Proof, requirement of the "Testimony of Claimant," reveals that:

–Character of Land: It is hard wood timber, farming land.

–Kind of Timberland, etc.: Beech, maple, hemlock and cedar.

It was also said that this homesteader had a wife and six children.

About 1878, the value was $300.00 for the 160 acres and a 16′ X 24′ log house with two doors, three windows, a shingle roof, and a board floor; barn 28′ X 58′; stable 20′ X 30′.

Farm Implements: Plough, harrow, 3 axes, 2 chains, 2 saws, and owned for five years.

Domestic Animals on Farm: One yoke or oxen, 2 cows, 2 heifers, 12 pigs, and 20 chickens.

Articles of Furniture: 4 beds, one table, 6 chairs, one stove, and necessary household goods.

Then the questions were:

How many seasons and crops raised? It was answered with five seasons, and wheat, rye, oats, barley, potatoes, and C (which is for corn).

Question No. 39 was "Are the improvements on this land assessed for taxes?" And it was answered very politely with "No. sir."

With all the answers required, the government "red tape" required a shrewd mind, which the homesteaders possessed.

Testimony of witness was usually a neighbor farmer, with a spirit of cooperation, as the Germans testified for the Poles, and vice versa. Example, if the subsequent homesteader was Polish, the testimony of two German witnesses, and two Polish witnesses. The ethnic differences were forgotten by the homesteaders because they were in a tough environment.

Questions presented to the witnesses were:

Q. How far from the residence of the claimant do you live, and how long have you lived there?

A. 5½ miles, and 9 years.

Q. How long have you known the claimant?

A. Various answers were given. Usually from a five to nine year period.

Q. How often have you been on this land, that is: Claimants, at what time or times, and when did you last see him on the land?

A. About 75 times, at all seasons of the year.

Q. State specifically the character of this land.

A. Timber land of no value, only for farming purposes.

Q. What is this land worth, that is 160 acres about 1878?

A. About $550.00.

Q. What is raised?

A. Wheat, rye, oats, peas, barley, potatoes, hay and garden stuff.

With questions like these to be answered, there was tranquility in the farming communities.

The first witness was 50 years of age, and of German extraction. The Polish claimant was 40 years of age.

A second witness, of German extraction, being 30 years of age, was very succint in his answers, and a few examples are given.

Q. What timber, etc.?

A. It is hard wood.

Question 25, asked: "How much of said land has been broken, how much plowed since being broken, and how much put into crop each season? State kinds of crops raised, their value, and number of seasons crops were raised?"

In answer, it was said: "15 acres; 15 acres, 1st year cropped 2 acres; 2nd year, 5 acres; 3rd year, 7 acres; 4th, 11 acres; 5th, 15 acres." Then he continued with "wheat, oats, peas, barley, potatoes, rye, and garden stuff."

These were educated, rugged, hard-working homesteaders, and their independence, self-reliance, continuous self-education and other personable personality traits, enriched this state, so the question of whether homesteads should be made available today even if only five acres, to make the residents self-sufficient in part, is something that should be considered.

48
CENTENNIAL ORATION

Of all the orations and sermons given in Michigan for the Centennial, it is the writer's opinion that the greatest was given at Bay City, Michigan, by Judge Isaac Marston, who then was Judge of the Supreme Court.

The preparation for the Centennial in the Bay City area was lukewarm and indifferent and, in fact, they almost abandoned the idea of any celebration. There was in that part of Michigan a vast body of foreign citizens who were patriots, and some considered foreign even though citizenship had been obtained. These foreign immigrants were the ones who with their various civic societies initiated a celebration worthy of the Centennial of 1876. As that day arrived, Bay City was loaded with these so-called foreign citizens and they were there to hear Judge Marston speak because they appreciated the blessings that they had enjoyed in this great state.

Judge Marston started off his speech, which was very appropriate for the occasion, by stating that it was the work of Thomas Jefferson which led to the Declaration of Independence. Judge Marston said the founding of this nation was not the work of any one man but a spontaneous development of free principles. He stated that this "germ" of free principles was nurtured in oppressions. He then traced the operation of the political and moral causes and mentioned how difficulties and adverse circumstances developed the heroes and statesmen in this country. He then mentioned George Washington and the Civil War which brought out Grant and Lincoln.

Judge Marston then stated that there was no danger which would threaten this country, and he came to the conclusion that the United States was in no danger of foreign conquest or oppression.

With all of the foreigners and foreign societies in attendance, here the speaker addressed himself more particularly to these so-called foreign groups. These foreign societies invited him to make the address in Bay City, Michigan, showing the people how they participated as American citizens while still cherishing some affection for their native lands.

He appealed to the Frenchmen by the memory of Lafayette. He appealed to the Polanders by the memory of Kosciusko, the patriot soldier of two continents, and by the memories of Poland's own heroic struggle for freedom. A well-read judge, he brought up the Insurrection of 1830 and 1831 and then he stressed the 1863 Insurrection in Poland. It was this Insurrection that brought so many of the Polish people to the State of Michigan.

The judge drew a glowing picture of the gallant conduct and the proud record of the German, French, Polish, and Irish soldiers in the Civil War, and remarked that America had the best blood of every land to defend her. He continued with stating that the blood of foreign-born citizens lay comingled with that of Americans on every battle-field. He continued to state that the loyalty of our adopted citizens was, and must always remain, unquestioned.

The gifted orator then spoke about the then delicate ground of the so-called Mongolian question. This Mongolian question was whether the Chinese should be allowed to come to America. Judge Marston rebuked the spirit of persecution which was manifested toward the Chinese on the Pacific Coast. He mentioned the scope of legislation and stated that the Chinese should be prevented from importation to this country for only servile or immoral purposes. He continued and stated that if the United States could not civilize and Christianize the few Mongolians that came here, America ought to surrender the proud boast of enlightenment and power.

The judge then alluded to the school question and stated that our public school system was the foundation or our liberties. He cautioned that we should be aware of any steps of the Union of the Church and State because it is inconsistent with our liberties. This learned judge was a prophet because over a century ago he realized that the German, Polish, Irish, and French, who were then considered foreign citizens, assimilated into America very easily and today constitute a great proportion of native Americans.

This Bicentennial was no different than the Centennial year of over a century ago. There were many groups that were lukewarm and indifferent.

As stated before, during the Bicentennial there was many orations and sermons but the question remains: Did the Bicentennial produce an oration that was founded with the wisdom and had the foresight of Judge Marston of the Supreme Court of Michigan?

49
POLISH PROOF–88%

It was an informative revelation to read the complete 1880 census records of the Township of Posen, County of Presque Isle, State of Michigan, from the National Archives records.

In 1879 and 1880, Michigan was in a recession. Furthermore, in the summer of 1880, Michigan had a flu epidemic. The records indicate that not one person was ill in the Township of Posen, which today is separated into the Township of Posen and the Township of Pulaski.

The census was taken between the period of June 1 to June 26 in the year 1880.

The enumerator was a Henry Clothier, an attorney in Rogers City, Michigan, then an attorney in Alpena, Michigan. Clothier was married to Carolyn Molitor, she being the sister of the notorious Albert Molitor, who was a con man, the biggest liar in northeastern Michigan, and who was court-martialed while serving in the U.S. Army for stealing a government horse. This is recounted in another article.

Even though it was a depression year, the Village of Posen had a saloon and, of course, a priest.

Unless a person has a knowledge of Polish, the census reports are a little complicated. Furthermore, the Posen area centennial book mentions many of the Polish names in the original Polish.

Since the enumerator did not know Slavic and/or German languages, many of the names were spelled phonetically. He made a few understandable errors, such as listing George for Albert.

The total number of residents in the census was 857. Of these 857 people, 756 persons, or 88% of the persons residing in this area, were of Polish extraction.

Of these 756 persons, the enumerator listed 40% of these persons as being born in German Prussia. The reason for stating that they were born in Prussia is that the Provinces of Poznan, Silesia, Pomerania, and Danzig were taken by the Prussian Government.

In this census group were 95 Germans being from Saxony, Hanover, Wurtenberg, but most listed Prussia. There were three French Canadians, and one Canadian had a wife born in England.

It is to be noted that one Pole, a Matthew Jezewski, was born in Holland, as were his parents. Holland had a Polish settlement after the Insurrection of 1830.

The area had 499 children (18 years and under, even though 21 years of age at that time constituted majority), or 58% of the community were children, who also toiled the soil.

A daughter of Peter Zapczynski was born in Quebec in 1867. The reason this is mentioned is that many of the Polish people who eventually settled in Presque Isle County embarked at Hamburg or Bremen, Germany, arriving in Quebec City, which trend started during the Civil War due to the alleged Blockade. It is to be noted that two children were born in New York, possibly the mother giving birth on the ocean or on Ellis Island after the lengthy ocean voyage.

Many of the children were born in Wisconsin and Ohio, a few in Pennsylvania. Most of the children were born in Michigan or Indiana.

A Polish man was married to a German woman, which was not uncommon at that time of history.

As was stated before, none of the inhabitants were ill and they were all very healthy. The records reveal that there was a thirteen-year-old boy who was a mute.

The total families for this community numbered 173. There were twelve widows and two widowers. There were 12 children in school during the census year, one being the writer's uncle by his marriage to a maternal aunt.

One of the widows was Anna Eschke, age 37, the housekeeper of Father Bogacki. Another widow listed was a Michaline Witucki, age 56, her husband being killed by a falling tree on his homestead in 1871, and she being one of the first women in the village, and a great-great aunt of the writer of this chapter.

According to the enumerator, there were no marriages during the census year, June 1, 1879 to May 31, 1880. Other records reveal two weddings during this period for this area. Probably the enumerator did not inquire because of his lack of ability to speak another language.

There were no divorced persons in this community. The first divorce granted in Presque Isle County was on August 18, 1872, to Lucille Molitor against Albert Molitor, the "monarch" of the lumber barons (Bentley Historical Library, Ann Arbor).

The National Archives record reveals that the majority of the adults listed could read and write, and it is known that these homesteaders could read and write both German and Polish.

Item 14 of the census report asks the question: "Number of months this person has been unemployed during the census year?" They were all employed and none of the adults listed were out of work for any period of time, including the Catholic priest and the saloon keeper. During that census year, persons employed in the cities researched (Detroit, for example) were laid off for at least six months, without any unemployment compensation.

In item 15 of the census report it has reference to health, and this question is asked: "Is the person (on the day of the enumerator's visit) sick, or temporarily disabled, so as to be unable to attend to ordinary business or duties? If so, what is the sickness or disability? Of all the residents listed, there was no person ill at the time of the census in June 1880.

The oldest couple listed in the report was Martin Lowinski, age 89, and his wife Anna, age 79, who were the parents of Catherine Lewandowski. These senior citizens resided with their two daughters and a son, along with the obedient grandchildren.

During the census year there were 44 children born, including a set of twins, Mary and Michael Gabrysiak, who were born on October 12, 1879, but taken to Detroit that winter (census records, 1880, Detroit) and confirmed as the twins were relatives of the writer.

In addition to the set of twins listed above, there were five sets of twins living in the area in June of 1880. The twins were: Anthony and Pauline Feder, age 6, who were born in Michigan; Martha and Catherine Smosh (Smarszcz), age 6, born in Ohio; Peter and Paul Lewinduski (Lewandowski), age 6, born in Michigan; Joseph and Peter Pretzebella (Przybyla), age 5, born in Michigan; and Michael and Mary Pelaski (Pilarski), age 4, who were born in Michigan.

The most common name for the women and daughters was Mary and Anna; for the men and sons it was Joseph and John. Many of the families had sons and daughters named Joseph and Josephine; Paul and Pauline; Frank and Frances; Michael and Michaline.

Many of the masculine names were Simon, Adam, Ignatz (Ignatius), Valentine, Isadore, Constantine, Teofil, Jacob, Dominic, Mathias, and Lawrence.

Female names in that era of history were: Constance, Matilda, Sally, Pelagia, Christina, Magdalene, Augustina, Justina, and Leokadia.

It should be noted that the first name of Hieronim was not listed in all of the names. However, there was one person listed as Herman.

The size of the families varied, usually from four to six children. The largest family was the family of Michael Wait (Wojt). He had seven children in his family when daughter Victoria was born in November 1879. All of the seven children were born either in Michigan or in the State of Indiana. When Mathias Scheminsky, a widower, with two sons, married Frances (nee Pawlak) Wojtych, a widow, with two daughters, they then had three more children. A person wonders how tranquility was maintained in a cabin, with seven children, no radio or television. The writer was not as prolific as his great-grandmother, Frances.

It must have been quite an experience for the enumerator who did not understand the Polish and German language, with their unique customs. Undoubtedly when making this census, the enumerator had his luncheon and dinner served to him by the generous Poles and Germans who believed in good food. Whether the enumerator ate any of the spiced fresh kielbasa, the head cheese, herring (*sledzie*), the fresh churned butter, and Polish bagels would only be conjecture, but there were no carry outs in that time of history.

Clothier must have been amazed when he saw all of the clucking hens with their chicks near the homesteaders' barns. As the enumerator crossed the many streams and rivers in the area, he must have been greeted by the ducks that were around; but he really must have been on guard when he saw all the geese that the Poles raised for their festive meals and, of course, for the goose grease that was saved for the high top leather boots and, of course, for the goose grease application on the chest during the time of colds. The Poles raised these geese in order to save the down from which was made the comforter (*pierzyna*), in addition to the other uses.

The enumerator knew the time by the sound of the melodious bells of the big Polish church. He quit at six in the evening, at which time the residents ate another substantial meal. Where he bedded down can be determined from the last entry of the day.

Yes, it should be mentioned that the Poles made their own wine, brandy and home brew beer. But their specialty was *spirytus* which had to be made for the Polish festivities and also for medicinal purposes. The writer vividly recalls "finding" such *spirytus* in the granary of a relative's farm while at a wedding reception. After one "swig," all of the youngsters were running to the pumpwell for the cold water. And, of course, this alcohol was 88% proof, coinciding with 88% of the Polish population in the then Township of Posen as enumerated in the census report of 1880 that was obtained from the National Archives in Washington, D.C.

50
THE FIRST EDUCATIONAL VIOLENCE

The original black versus white fight in Posen, Michigan, was the divergence of opinion of the homesteaders. This divergence was to the issue regarding building a school with a library, as against a church. The black group (intellectuals) lost, and the community built a church, not a school of science.

On June 15, 1874, Father Francis X. Schulak (Shulak), S.J., of Saint Ignatius College, Chicago, Illinois, purchased forty acres of land, adjacent to the present Saint Casimer's Church at Posen, Michigan, from the County Clerk, Frederich Denny Larke, and the State of Michigan. The $100.00 (in gold coins) invested by the Jesuit was for a possible museum, library and college, in the NORTH WOODS OF MICHIGAN, a dream and wish of the vigorous missionary.

Father Schulak arrived at Alpena in 1870 and spoke to the Polish foresters who were buying material for the construction of their cabins and barns on their homesteads in the present Posen area. He was very impresseive in stature, at 5′11″ tall (average height then being 5′4″), dark in complexion, "salt and pepper" hair, blue eyes, with a high forehead, long nose, oval-shaped chin, a medium-sized mouth (but a good orator), and an oval face (Department of State Archives). He could speak, read and write in English, Polish, Latin, German, Czech and French, so wherever he went, his missionary assignments were well received and appreciated.

The Jesuit planned and founded libraries in all of his

parishes, from Missouri to Buffalo, New York. The libraries he founded were to be the center of education of the Polish people, and called "The Libary of the Good Book" (*Writings* of *Francis Domanski, S.J.*).

All of the Poles wanted a school and library to further the education of the Polish and Bohemian immigrants. (It was a novelty in America at that time to have a library in a parish).

The intellectual Jesuit and the educated Polish people in Posen (they could read and write in German and Polish, and corresponded in Gothic German, which is basically Latin) were of the opinion that every newcomer should be handed a good, religious written book and a popular magazine in Polish. He obtained books from Poland and the village correspondent, Frances (nee Pawlak) Wojtych Szymanska (Scheminsky), subscribed to the Sacred Heart Messenger, then written in Polish.

To fight ignorance and illiteracy, Schulak's weapons were the Holy Scripture and a good book.

Schulak wanted to establish a museum of science on the forty acres in Posen like the one he established in Chicago. He collected mineral stones, colorful butterflies and other insects. He stuffed birds and animals for the Chicago Museum and the museums in Europe. The Posen correspondent's daughter, Salomia, received a stuffed owl from the saintly Jesuit, who could imitate various bird and animal calls.

The Jesuit also wanted to establish in Posen a school of botany, mineralogy, and zoology. He wanted a college in the north, due to the natural surroundings and the last virgin forests.

With this in mind, the early land owners, named Kowalski, Szymanski, Kufel, Loshinski, Strelecki, Muszynski, Gabrysiak, Bronikowski, Skowronek, Dojas, Gappa, Jachik, Konwinski, Krol, Kujawa, Nowicki, Shoola, Przybyla, Purgill, Semp, Woloszyk, Wiza, Zabczynski, and others, wanted the school, and they directed Frances Szymanski to write a letter to the Bishop that they wanted "Jesuits" to be in charge of the parishioners' spiritual and educational needs (National Archives, Names).

After a few years, the Bishop responded by ignoring the properous community citizens (they were all naturalized by then), and sending a secular priest, not an order priest. The secular priest, no comparison to the intellectual Jesuit, never was accepted by the Polish community.

Father Anthony Bogacki, age 31, arrived in Posen in 1879, and Bogacki immediately changed the nine year plans of the homesteaders, who were willing to build a school and library.

Bogacki hired a servant, which the parishioners vehemently objected to, as they figured the priest could do his own housekeeping. The priest in his daily walk would stop and talk to the saloon keeper, John Stosik, age 29, and the two of them concluded that a huge church would attract people. At that time, Stosik had just arrived from Prussia (Poland) with his wife, Mary, age 18, and was not of the original group. Stosik had no children at the time, so he and the priest "pushed" for a church, while most of the Poles, educated in Poland, wanted a school for their children born here in America (Age, etc., National Archives).

The secular priests at that time were considered old-fashioned, under-educated for the position, and conservative clergy, so Father Bogacki named the pro-school persons "BLACK," after the black-robed Jesuits, especially Father Schulak, who wanted a school of science.

This divergence of opinion caused violence not only around the church grounds but many fights at Polish weddings, etc., where everybody was invited to all festivities.

In 1876, Father Schulak was seen as a strange innovator, a radical, and a suspicious priest by many persons who met him, and especially by the German and Irish Bishops, but a century ahead of his time.

In 1976, after the Second Ecumenical Council, the saintly Father Schulak would be recognized as a "good priest with predicable vision" (from *THE SAILING MISSIONARY*, by Natsolim).

If Father Francis X. Schulak (Sulak, Szulak, Shulak), S.J., had had his way, would there today be a POSEN INSTITUTE OF TECHNOLOGY?

THE GENERAL STORE

Mrs. Zabawka, a daughter of homesteaders, placing her order with one of the partners at the general store. Note the other partner and employee. The delivery man, attired in full coat, is absorbing the heat from the pot-bellied stove. The hardwood floor indicates a general store, as butcher shops in the nineteenth century had sawdust on the floor.

Notice the milk buckets, buggy whips, brooms, and scale. Also the baking powder cans, cookies, bread, graham wafers, home made cookies, and the vanilla extract bottles.

Identify the cracker barrel, pickle barrel, salt-herring barrel, brown sugar barrel, egg container, and the prune box.

Mittens, caps, gloves, tobacco pipes, kerosene lamps and cans were all obtainable at this exclusive general store.

51
THE POLISH PLANTATION

At the Detroit, Michigan, Land Office on April 22, 1870, a Kasimer (Casimer) Kulich paid $14.00 under application number 795 (National Archives) for 160 acres of land, which Kulich envisioned as a plantation. The land was the SE¼ of Section 5, 33N, Range 6 East, presently in Posen Township, Michigan, the corner of North Grand Lake Highway and Hincka Road.

The 1871 and 1872 crops were successful on the virgin soil, especially after the huge forest fires of 1868, which fertilized the soil.

His 1873 experimental crop having failed, Kasimer relinquished the land to the United States. It was on September 24, 1873, at Detroit that he "acknowledged the foregoing relinquishment to be his free act and deed" before Thomas S. Day, a Wayne County, Michigan, Notary Public, employed by the Land Office (National Archives).

That autumn Kulich explained the property to a Polish resident in Wayne County and the potential of the started tobacco plantation. The enterprising Kulich also explained the Homestead Act for a fee.

The subsequent homesteader on January 24, 1874, settled on the land, being quaranteed that all tobacco raised would be purchased by Kasimer Kulich, who also encouraged the Poles in Detroit to homestead in Posen.

Kulich would inform the Land Office of any abandonment for a fee, as the example of abandonment by Joseph Pinkowski of Branch County, Michigan, who arrived with

Jacob Strzelecki and obtained 160 acres of land in Section 28 and 29 of the present Pulaski Township on April 16, 1870, at the Detroit Land Office under application No. 781. Pinkowski's signature was in the old German script (National Archives, Washington, D.C.).

A publication in the ALPENA COUNTY PIONEER, from August 8, 1872, to September 12, 1872, where A. C. Tefft was the publisher of the weekly publication and an A. J. Keller was the Notary Public, had reference to this land. The publication of the complaint of abandonment of his homestead was for the cancellation of the Homestead Entry No. 781, as Pinkowski "has not cleared, fenced, cultivated, built upon, or in any way improved said Land . . . That he is not now residing upon, and has not resided upon said Land since the date of entry." Kulich further testified on September 16, 1872, that the "residence of the locater being unknown to me, a personal service of notice to appear in this case was impracticable." Affidavit at the Land Office was signed by Jan Sweda and termed a "Contested Homestead Entry" (National Archives).

Pinkowski's homestead was finally cancelled for abandonment on June 9, 1876.

The original homesteader of Wayne County was more of a "huckster" than a farmer; but he envisioned being the "gentry" of the Michigan Tobacco Plantations, so he selected his tobacco seeds with scrutiny, as did the subsequent homesteader of his original entry of his homestead land.

It can be assumed that it was the dark and unstemmed tobacco that was raised on this land from 1874 to 1879, as in the testimony of witness Lorenz Kowalski dated February 17, 1879, before Frederich Denny Larke, County Clerk. Also grown on the twenty acres of fenced and cultivated land was wheat, oats, corn, rye, potatoes, hay, general garden vegetables, and, of course, tobacco.

After harvest, the tobacco was air-cured (aged). It was grated by a rasp, then flavored. Rasping (or grinding) one's own tobacco would make it fresh. It could then be flavored or moistened. The rasp was part of the homesteader's whittling knife at that time.

A mortar and pestle was used by the women to grind tobacco for their husbands and fathers, and sometimes the women themslves used it for medicinal purposes, as in Europe among the "European Aristocracy." Different types of perfume could be added, and, of course, cedar. Mustard seed was grown and used; and when ground and mixed with the snuff, the sneezing would echo to Lake Huron.

In coarse powder form, it was sniffed into each nostril by the thumb and forefinger. Medical varieties and home varieties were made. Snuff was used for the treatment of colds and to make a person sweat.

If there was a bad tobacco crop, tree leaves would be cut and cured, usually from a leaf that was dark, and such leaves were mixed with the tobacco.

The snuff was contained in a wooden case with an ivory opener, the style of the time.

The snuff tickled the nose; then blowing the nose; and then wiping the nose. This was the way to consume their leisure time, as today in watching T.V., or if a person was bored, or in the "doldrums."

The writer vividly recollects the hot summer of 1933 when he attended church with his paternal grandfather. The visiting clergyman in his sermon was testing the endurance of the hard-working Poles, with his lengthy continuous sermon (hell and women, or does it make a difference), on that hot sultry Sunday. The village elders, with some pre-arranged signal, took out their snuff boxes, pinched an amount, passed the box to the right and left (usually sons, grandsons, etc.), and everybody sniffed the then commercially sold snuff. About ninety seconds later, the whole congregation sneezed. The clergyman rapidly descended the pulpit, and shortly thereafter the services were abruptly concluded.

Yes, it is believable that the snuff-sneezing echo was heard from Posen to Rogers City, Alpena, and possibly across Lake Huron to the Georgian Bay area.

The envisioned Posen Polish Plantation was "snuffed out," when the homesteader's children commenced using commercially sold snuff, which today, if used, would prompt some organization to begin a rally to "SNUFF OUT SNUFF."

52
ABANDONED HOMESTEADS

Persons applying under the Homestead Act in northeastern Michigan in the County of Alpena and Presque Isle County had only to pay $14 for 160 acres, but with this 160 acres came a lot of grief and many of the homesteaders abandoned their homesteads and returned to Wayne County and Branch County, Michigan, and also to St. Joseph County and Noble County, Indiana.

When a homesteader made an application he stated that this application "is made for the purpose of actual settlement and cultivation, that said entry is made for my exclusive use and benefit and not directly or indirectly for the use or benefit of any other person or persons whomsoever."

As with any government agency, in a new homesteader that was to follow, there were more forms to be filled out by the new homesteader and also more restrictions.

One of the restrictions was that "timber land embraced in a homestead, or other entry not consummated, may be cleared in order to cultivate the land and improve the premises, *but for no other purpose*.

If after clearing the land for cultivation, there remains more timber than is required for improvement, there is no objection to the settler disposing of the same. But, the question whether the land is being cleared of its timber *for legitimate purposes* is a question *of fact* which is liable to be raised at any time. If the timber is cut and removed *for any other purpose* it will subject the entry to cancellation, and the person who cut it will be *liable to civil suit* for recovering of the value of said timber, *and also to criminal prosecution* under Section 2461 of the revised statute."

If any of the rugged homesteaders would have taken these paragraphs seriously it would have taken another fifty years for anyone to homestead that land under such ridiculous limitations.

It is a known fact that the homesteaders had to sell part of the lumber in order to purchase the necessities of live, such as clothes, leather, salt, pepper, other spices, and incidentals.

Three persons from Branch County, Michigan, namely Jacob Strelecki, Michael Dojas, and a Joseph Pinkowski, on April 6, 1870, applied at the Land Office in Detroit wherein each one obtained a homestead of 160 acres. One of these homesteads, which was never toiled, that is, of Joseph Pinkowski, required an affidavit of publication which was published for four weeks commencing in August 1872 by the publisher of the Alpena County Pioneer, a newspaper published and circulated in said county of Alpena once in each week. The publication, which ran for four weeks, stated that on August 6, 1872, at the United States Land Office, Detroit, Michigan, the register and receiver stated: "complaint having been entered at this office against Joseph Pinkowski for abandonment of his homestead, entry number 781, dated April 6, 1870, of Section 28, [which is presently in Pulaski Township.] With a view to the cancellation of said entry, the said parties are hereby summoned to appear at this office on the 16th day of September, 1872, at 10 o'clock a.m. to respond and furnish testimony concerning said alleged abandonment."

On September 16, 1872, one Kasimer Kulich of Presque Isle County, Michigan, appeared before the receiver in Detroit and he, being duly sworn according to law, did dispose and say that he resided in Township 33 North,

Range 6 East, and have for about two years past been well acquainted with the homestead land of Pinkowski, which was in Section 28, Township 34, Range 6 East, stating that Pinkowski entered under the Homestead Act on the sixth day of April 1870. Kulich went on to say "and I know from personal observation and examination that the said Joseph Pinkowski has not cleared, fenced, cultivated, built upon, or in any way improved said land; that he is not now residing upon and has not resided upon said land since the date of the entry. Further, that the residence of the locater being unknown to me, a personal service of notice to appear in this case was impractical."

A Jan Sweda, residing in Wayne County, was the translator, and he stated that Kasimer Kulich knew the contents of the said affidavit relative to the abandonment of the homestead entry of Joseph Pinkowski, and from Sweda's personal observation the statements therein need to be true according to the statements made by Kasimer Kulich.

It is not ironical because Kasimer Kulich who was homesteading in Section 5 of Posen Township, on the 24th day of September 1873 in the County of Wayne, State of Michigan, stated that "I Kasimer Kulich do hereby relinquish to the United States all my right, title and interest of, in and to the land described in the within certificate." It was witnessed by a notary public who stated that on the 24th day personally appeared before the notary public Kasimer Kulich and acknowledged the foregoing release, it being his free act and deed.

Kulich returned to Wayne County, Michigan, and it is alleged that Pinkowski did not return to Branch County but he went to Chicago where employment was obtained.

The contested homestead entry according to the National Archives was finally cancelled for abandonment on June 9, 1876.

Many of the homesteaders, due to economic reasons or

the diminishing supply of timber in the St. Joseph Valley of Michigan and Indiana, decided to go to Presque Isle County where they could simultaneously be foresters, farmers, and homesteaders.

Whether it was the severe winter of 1870-71 or other factors would only be conjecture or speculation, but it is known that many of the homesteaders who stayed on such land for five years were rugged individuals. It is known in life many attempts are made for betterment and independence but over half are abandoned.

POWEDZIENA !

53
CATALOG DREAMLAND

When the children and grand-children of the Polish homesteaders in northeastern Michigan could not attend school due to a heavy snow storm and the "mountainous" snow drifts, then there was leisure time for such children.

After completing the chores of watering all the animals, then feeding the chickens and geese, "oatsing" and "haying" the beast of burden, slopping the pigs, plus "mashing" the milk cows, it was back to the living room for the children.

Relaxing on bearskin or sheepskin rugs around the mammoth potbellied heating stove, their "dreaming" commenced, as they fingered the various catalogs.

Each family in that era of history always requisitioned all the available catalogs to determine the latest fashions, and to purchase the necessities which were not available in their communities.

Looking through these catalogs, the children visualized what the city "dudes" were purchasing and wearing, and they were self-educating themselves by reading each item that was advertised and illustrated.

The children with their practical demands knew that most items for sale could never be procured, as it was an economic impossibility for their parents, but "kids" do dream.

After teaching themselves the farm implements and supplies, plus the clothes, they would go to the toy section and items of new patents and discoveries, such as the new and various electrical gadgets (there was no Rural Electrification in that period of history).

During many long dark autumn evenings the candles (and later the kerosene lamps) would be used, reading each page. Some of the smarter children could quote item and page number better than verse and chapter of the Bible.

When the latest issues of the catalogs were received, then the old catalogs had another use. Each sheet of the catalog was used then, comparable to each tissue that is used from a box of Kleenex today.

The boys especially would imitate their fathers by placing numerous sheets in their pocket in the event of a necessity. Such sheets were used when on a fishing trip, catching frogs, "fetching" the cows, berry or mushroom picking, or near the swimming hole (which was usually a stream, pond, or river).

Certain pages of the catalogs were saved for cut-outs, especially by the girls who had the priority to use the items in the clothes mending kit.

The girl's imagination was amazing. Grandma would mix the flour-water paste, provide unused lined writing paper, and then she would act as advisor to the would-be designers and home planners.

Grandma would always explain "risque" words found in the catalog, words that were unacceptable to the parents in that period of the phony Victorian era.

Painting of these cutouts was accomplished as Grandma always concocted various colors from her "secret formula," of various juices and fluids from produce, roots, etc.

All of these cutouts which were then considered "artistic" masterpieces would then be taken to school by the community girls and be placed on exhibition for the benefit of all of the other students.

Today many children "waste" their time in school on such masterpieces, forced to take such masterpieces home by the teacher–then the "silent suffering" by the parents in their admiration.

What was done in home a century ago today is done in school.

Back in that era of history of the one room school house, had many benefits but discipline was self-maintained by the various aged students in attendance.

Subsequently, the grandchildren and great grandchildren of these homesteaders who believed in educating their children at home in addition to the compulsory education, became outstanding students at many universities.

They became politicians, bishops, pathologists, news reporters, surgeons, dentists, electronic engineers, biologists, educators. One homesteading family produced two attorneys. All this was achieved through self-discipline and self-education, to a large extent.

This discipline was first established in the provinces of Poznan, Pomerania, Gdansk, and Silesia, where the written books were appreciated, read, and explained. This is part of the Polish heritage that has extended to the sixth generation Poles here in the Great Lakes area.

54
THE POLISH NEWSPAPERS

When the Poles settled in various parts of Michigan, other than Wayne County, they read German newspapers in addition to the imported Polish books until a Polish-American paper was established in the Middle West.

The Poles were always liberal and progressive, an example of that being that the Poles in the 1876 Presidential election at Presque Isle County voted Democratic even though many of the other ethnic groups voted Republican. This voting was possibly due to their spirit of cooperation which they were trained in due to their domination by the Prussian and Austrian Government and their individualistic traits which showed in their opposition to the conservative German editorials.

These new citizens wanted a "liberal" newspaper as they vehemently opposed the cartels they knew in Europe. The Poles always objected to monopolies, as they were independent by nature. They finished any business ventures that they started. This was shown by their endurance as homesteading farmers.

In the 1880's the village "librarian," a woman who was educated in Poland and read all of the available material, subscribed by mail for a Polish newspaper.

The newspaper, *Polski Kuryer*, appealed to the Poles from the Poznan, Pomeranian, and Silesian Provinces, as the editor of the newspaper was educated in the Poznan province.

This Polish newspaper's general theme was the lack of

representation of Poles in positions in employment with the governmental agencies, certain employment, and no representation in the hierarchy of the Catholic Church in America–the Church, which they supported. Their contribution, which percentagewise was in greater proportion than any other ethnic group, was known by the bishops, but the bishops ignored the "cry in the wilderness" of the Polish citizens.

This group of Poles, possibly similar to the Dissidents of a century earlier, intended to stay in America. They realized that they needed representation; otherwise, they would be ignored as were their Dissident ancestors.

These Poles knew that they had to stay in America as the majority departed Prussia in order to eliminate the conscription service which was raised to four years, and the Poles had no intention of wasting four years of their lives for the silly Prussian rulers who insisted on "war mongering."

They came to America for freedom and representation and they wanted such freedom and representation.

In their villages they all attended the weddings and other festivities as well as other Church activities. The spirit of cooperation prevailed, especially in a time of calamity. In a tough environment they had to cooperate to perpetuate their rugged, individualistic kind.

Their fervor for certain religious rules and edicts were observed in Michigan. The writer recollects that the Lenten Wednesday service of "*Gorzke Zale*," wherein the entire congregation sang, was almost an impossibility for the youngsters in attendance. Everyone observed the fast and abstinence, and the smell of the marinated herring and the smell of the raw onions would burn the young sensitive nostrils. The Sunday afternoon or evening services had the fragrance of kielbasa. The Friday lengthy Stations of the Cross had their aroma of fried fish combined with smoked fish. The Poles in that part of Michigan always believed in good food, and in America such good food was more than abundant.

The "informed" men of the Polish village would discuss their latest interpretation of the Polish newspapers. The newspaper subscribers would inform the non-readers of the latest trend in America. In fact, they were in agreement that Polish should be taught at public schools similar to Latin and Greek, even though such request was ignored by the WASP faction that controlled the education system.

The conservative non-readers objected to such "nonsense," saying that this would diminish the parochial schools. The Polish progressives even advocated the teaching of German in public schools. (It should be noted that in that era of history the Germans had their own parochial schools–usually the minister was the headmaster.)

Advocating such "liberalism" grouped the Polish and German progressives in the village against the Polish and German "status quo," who objected to any type of change, even a change of modern agricultural methods. This divergence at times led to violence, in addition to the bickering among the youngsters at school. The teachers, in their forced neutrality, resigned and transferred to larger communities where difference of opinion was tolerated.

This difference did not end when the pastor of the congregation informed his parishioners that they could not read a certain Polish newspaper, otherwise the non-Polish bishop would excommunicate such parishioners. The village parishioners recalled themselves or were informed of the time in Posen, Poznan, Poland, when the archbishop of Poznan agreed to a Prussian rule which stated that no Polish songs be sung in Prussian Poland, including any church songs. The bishop's directive was not adhered to and laughed at, similar to what their parents did of the archbishop of Poznan who tried to curtail Polish songs.

The Bishop's pastoral letters were read to the congregation by the obedient priest. Then came the showdown.

On a Palm Sunday, the village priest had to inform the congregation that no absolution would be given for the required yearly confession to persons subscribing to a certain Polish newspaper. He further informed the parishioners that a meeting would follow the High Mass.

After the High Mass all the women departed—then began the argument. Only the priest presented the ban on the reading of this certain Polish newspaper. No parishioner seconded the priests's motion, nor did any other parishioner speak in favor of banning such newspaper.

Then the affable, most powerful elder in the community presented his long, logical oration regarding freedom of press and reasons for coming to America. It was seconded by the most prosperous parishioner.

The priest again read the pastoral letter of excommunication and at this meeting no wine was served as it was Lent and the Poles adhered to no drinking during Lent. After this meeting all but two of the leading citizens cancelled his subscription due to the pastoral letter and possibly fearful that they would not receive absolution.

The two leading citizens were always in demand by all of the villagers in order to hear the news of the so-called banned Polish publication.

The priest was transferred within a year so all the area citizens re-subscribed to the Polish newspaper.

The community was happy again. The farm children continued again their daily races. They would race each other on their way to pick up the newspapers at the village post office. The fastest horse was named "*Perki*" (potatoes in that version of Polish), owned by Pelasia, a blue-eyed, black-haired beauty of the surrounding area. Pelasia was also an accomplished concertina (accordian) player and was very temperamental. Sometimes the races would be held with sleighs, as that part of Michigan had a yearly heavy snowfall.

As history repeats, the Poles in Michigan today continue to read what they want to read, and as their ancestors did not pay any attention to the Archbishop of Poznan who tried to ban Polish songs in Polish churches, such banning has absolutely no value among the Poles who are readers of newspapers, periodicals, and good books.

CRYSTAL CLEAR COLD WATER

KLACH and *WALACH* were the names of the trained team of horses. The wagon conveyed four fifty gallon wooden barrels of water. The rivers and streams were clean and crystal clear providing water for all homesteaders, foresters, farmers and livestock. During a drought the water was used for irrigating the vegetables. Such streams were over abundant with speckled trout, considered the best tasting fish by the Poles in 1870.

POLISH POLO PLAYERS

In the picture, Grandpa is on the biggest horse, the lead horse, and in front of the horse is Kogut, the game rooster who was "boss" of the farm fowl. The clarinet player and violinist are to the right of the lead horse. The gray-haired woman in the entrance way of the house, between the third and fourth horses in the background, is the writer's great-grandmother who homesteaded the land in 1870.

55
POLISH POLO PLAYERS

In section 9 of Posen Township, Presque Isle County, Michigan (which is across the road from the Polish Church), in the summer of 1896, the polo game of the century was held for the homesteaders.

Polo was introduced in Michigan by the Polish people, due to their superior knowledge and experience as Polish Cavalry officers. This introduction commenced during the Civil War which coincided with the Polish Insurrection of 1863, when masses of Poles arrived in Michigan.

The origin of polo as to what civilization or country is not known. Polo is a Tibetan word *pulu*, meaning a ball. Genghis Khan played a variant of the game with a Mongolian type of pony. When Genghis invaded Poland, he introduced the King of Game, or Game of Kings. As Poland's land contour was primarily flat and fertile, horses were a necessity for toiling the soil and the military forces then being the excellent cavalry.

The modified version of polo as played then in Michigan had:

1. The polo field of 200 yards by 100 yards.
2. The ball was made of hand sewn saddle leather, stuffed with dried cured moss; four inches in diameter, but the weight of the ball was never recorded.
3. Polo sticks were made from pine wood, and these boards were 2½ inches wide, ¾ inch thick, and 48 inches long. These sticks were aged, sanded and treated similar to a baseball bat today.

4. Four men to a group (team). A good horseman was needed. The rider had to possess balance of himself, and expertise to balance the horse.

5. Draft horses. Some homesteaders had at least six horses. Draft horses of that era were used for plowing the fields, and in the winter for work in the lumber camps.

6. Referees, umpires, and goal judges were composed of the village elders who boasted of their youthful years as polo players. Their rules were:

A. No penalties for dangerous riding, as plow horses were used, hence, slow to start.

B. No penalties for rough handling and/or misuse of stick.

C. As the draft horses were sturdy and never fell or went lame, there was no horse disqualification.

The community children tallied the goals, even though the homesteaders' rules required no timekeepers. Each game would be played until the "polo sticks" were broken. Once broke, the player was out of the game, where he watched from the sideline. Each game would usually be under an hour, then the winning participants were given first chance at the home brew beer that was cooled in the artesian well.

The women would bring their picnic baskets and relax under the trees in the orchard. Baskets contained a Polish potato salad (with marjoram), bread, smoked dried kielbasa, green onions, and wild strawberries.

The men would mount their horses when the clarinet player and usually two violinists would play *Jeszce Polska Nie Zginela* in remembrance of Poland being partitioned by Prussia, Austria and Russia. This song always made the rugged Poles shed "silent" tears for their relatives in occupied Poland.

The lead horseman would then arch his left elbow to show the flat of his left extended hand. To the right, one length behind, would be the second player. Twenty feet to the right was the third player, who usually had the fastest horse in a gait. Seven feet to his right was the fourth player (oldest in age).

The *pilka* (ball) would be rolled to the center by the *sedzia* (umpire), and the competition commenced in a hilarious style.

There were various tricks that were played on the opponents. The grandfather of the writer would allow other persons to ride his specially trained horses. If there was a newcomer to the community, or a travelling salesman, such neophyte would be given a certain trained horse in order to participate in the game of the century on Grampa's polo field.

The novice would be allowed to play about 15 minutes before noon. He would be encouraged to ride the "lively" horse, and all the villagers in attendance would applaud this novice.

At about the time the visiting novice began feeling confident and appreciated, the huge church bells would ring for the noon angelus. Immediately the novice's trained horse would stop. His teammates would go to the novice's rescue, trying to encourage him to get the horse to move, so the game could continue. After five minutes of such humiliation for the novice, they all agreed that it was time for the noon banquet.

Such travelling salesman or other novice never did realize that Grandpa had this one horse trained to stop when the church bells rang at noon. This horse was trained to demand his oats, hay, and a yellow transparent apple (in season) when the noon bells were rung.

Grandpa won many beers and snuff with this trained horse, as nobody but Grandpa could get this horse to move after the church bells rang.

After the noon banquet, children of the village would mount all the horses at the farm polo field. These children would then form a huge circle in the field. In the center of the circle a bantam rooster would be released. Any participant catching the rooster, named *Kogut*, would be awarded a quarter eagle gold coin.

Kogut was entered for fourteen years before being retired. Grandma claimed the gold coin was "swallowed" by *Kogut*, as he never was caught.

Other informative reliable sources would testify that the gold coin was departed with in a saloon in Alpena, Michigan. The victorious "polo player" team travelled to Alpena to purchase some leather for making a *pilka* (ball), but in the process of negotiations at the saloon, it was proved that Kogut never did "swallow" the gold coin.

56
TALL AND LEAN

Sufficiency and variety of food in the area of the "crescent" adjoining and to the south of the Baltic Sea, through the generations had produced people who are tall and lean, and very seldom such people encounter the problem of obesity.

These people had basic rules, which complemented their region of sufficiency and variety of food.

One of the rules is that the women in that area did not marry until over 25 years of age, then usually to a man about 27 years of age. The reason was that the man had by then fulfilled his objectionable compulsory military service that was demanded by the Prussian rulers. At that age a man was established in a trade, business, or profession.

A basic rule is that all children were breast fed, and the women from that area are known for their firm full breasts, with large nipples. The breast feeding was accepted as part of nature, and it was common to see these women breast feeding their infants until the big depression. These women arrived in Michigan commencing in 1854 followed the basic rules until World War II when many changes were made, and such "foreign" natural rules were considered "old-fashioned."

Breast feeding from both full breasts prevented conception, which the women knew, and a family usually consisted of two to three children. Whether these women had another version of child planning was never recorded, but the women from that area were robust and enterprising, so some secret on child planning was known and handed down from generation to generation on the distaff side. This child planning secret was known as poksor.

The weaned child was then given foods that were mashed, after being boiled.

These Pomeranians, Poznanians, and Kashubs boiled most of their foods, soups having beef broth, chicken broth, and even fish soups, but most of the vegetable soups usually had a butter base.

Pork was not a basic diet of these people, but if used, the ribs would be boiled, then placed with saurkraut and potato dumplings (*kluski*). Pigs feet and knuckles would also be boiled for immediate consumption, otherwise pickled and smoked. Hams were always cured and smoked, and the other parts were made into a head cheese that could be stored.

Vegetables and fruits were consumed, as were a variety of cheeses. This combination was used on the many days that they fasted and abstained from meat or any meat derivative.

Even though the area produced sugar beets, sugar was sparingly used at times in their tea, but honey was so employed. Honey was also used for the cakes, cookies, and pies.

Seasoning usually consisted of a sour salt. Pepper was seldom used, as it had to be imported, and pepper in that era of history was usually contaminated.

The youngsters after the age of eight would not consume milk as it was considered only a "filler." Instead snacks would consist of radishes, celery, carrots, and cucumbers (in season); dill pickles, cold saurkraut, and sunflower seeds; hard-boiled eggs, an unsweetened version of a cookie, with natural preserves; and a bread with a piece of dried smoked beef (modern version of a beef jerky), consumed with a lot of sweet artesian well water. Berries and fruits were always used as a snack.

This group was trained never to be gluttonous (*zarloczny*), which training was perpetuated to the death bed, and this could be another reason for the leanness of this group. This tendency toward leanness was recorded prior to the year 1500, and such historical records stated that these people were four inches taller than the people in other parts of Europe in the year of 1500.

Artesian well water was consumed upon rising. Such water was used during the nightly cleaning of the teeth (massaging the gums with the finger and thumb, as there was no toothbrushes in that era of history) as well as a ladle full of artesian well water at bedtime.

The real secret to leanness, taught from generation to generation, was sufficient sleep. The theory being that if a small amount of food is consumed during any period (week to month), then more sleep is required, such as the period of the winter solstice.

Conversely, if the hours of labor were long and hard, then more food would be consumed, as in the summer months. This group has always been known to be hard workers.

Walking was always recommended. Even if a wagon or sleigh was used, a person should not sit on such wagon or sleigh for over a half hour, but walk alongside for a few minutes out of each half hour, thereby always having strong legs and good circulation.

Various roots, plants, and leaves were used for medicinal purposes, but such concoctions passed into oblivion, especially after arriving in the Great Lakes area where patent medicine could be purchased at the general store, at a medicine show, or from a travelling peddler.

At festivals or holidays, a home-made wine or brandy was consumed. Beer was very seldom drunk, even after the Prussian "Piracy" and tyranny, when the Prussians tried to impose beer upon the Poles instead of their home-made wine or brandy.

As most of this group were foresters, smoking was never considered. A version of Polish snuff was used, even when arriving in the Great Lakes area.

The theory of the ratio of sleep to food, food to sleep, has never been in practice in the Great Lakes area except by the fourth, fifth and sixth generations of these Poznanians, Pomeranians, and Kashubs, and this theory has had amazing results.

QUERIES: Is that theory in use by such descendants the reason these descendents to the sixth generation in the Great Lakes area are still tall and lean? Or, would these theories, if practiced enduringly by other persons, result in tall and lean people and there would never be the question of obesity?

57
MISCARRIAGE OF JUSTICE

In Volume One of the records of St. Albertus Church in Detroit, Michigan, it is revealed that a boy was born on May 28, 1874, and he was baptized in that parish on May 31, 1874.

It is alleged that he was born one month after his mother arrived from Prussian Poland.

When the inflation and the economic cycle was at its nadir from 1875, an event which lasted for over six years, on December 8, 1879, Paul Czolgosh, name as listed, applied for a state homestead in Section 30 of Krakow Township which is T-33 North, Range 7 East. The total amount of the homestead was 65 acres, situated in Presque Isle County, Michigan.

This land was patented or, in other words, the deed was obtained on September 23, 1885.

The church records in that period of time were destroyed by fire; however, it is known that in about 1889 Paul's son commenced working in the lumber camps in northeastern Michigan.

This went on until about 1894 when the lumbering industry was phasing out and people had to obtain employment in Detroit or Cleveland, Ohio.

It is the theory of the writer that Leon in about 1894 acquired a social disease either on the waterfront of Detroit or Cleveland. It should be stated that in the year 1900 there was no penicillin.

The social disease today would be considered neurosyphilis which involved the nervous system, consequently doing damage to the spinal cord and the brain tissue. When the spinal cord is attacked, there is a wasting away of the body, together with intense pain, incoordination and various peculiar sensations. Every doctor knows that paretic neurosyphilis invades the brain.

The tertiary syphilis relates to the central nervous system and this affliction begins with the subtle changes in the intellect, memory, mood, behavior and ending in psychosis.

While he was afflicted with this disease, on two different occasions Leon went to visit Emma Goldman. The reason for his contacting Emma Goldman was that she was a registered nurse. At that time in history, a registered nurse in the middle west had great power in dispensing medication. Leon, due to his brilliant mind and the amount of reading that he did, knew that if anybody would help him it would be Emma Goldman.

It is also the theory of the writer after numerous years of research–which research will continue after the Archives on Leon are open to the public–that Leon had high respect for law and order and he had no inclination to overthrow any government.

After firing the bullet at Buffalo, in 1901, Leon was brought to court. He was represented by two retired judges who did not do any defense trial work in excess of thirty years.

These defense attorneys did not even contact the alienists (alienist is comparable to psychiatrist today). Leon admitted to one of the alienists that he had a veneral disease.

During the time of the trial any of these alienists should have detected psychosis, otherwise, at the time of prior examining.

The trial and other facets of this article will be written at other times, but the records from the Department of

Correctional Services of the Auburn Correctional Facility in Auburn, New York, state that "Leon Czolgosz was received at Auburn State Prison, Auburn, New York, on September 27, 1901, and was subsequently electrocuted on October 29, 1901. He was sentenced in Erie County for the assassination of President William McKinley. It is also known that his alias was Fred Nieman."

After the electrocution a partial autopsy was performed. But there was no autopsy of the brain; hence, it could never be determined that he had neurosyphilis.

The Auburn Prison head clerk stated: "Although there are no written records indicating same, it has been said that this man was buried in the middle of the night in an unmarked location in Fort Hill Cemetery in this city. It was feared that his body would be exhumed by certain individuals who expressed great revenge and therefore those in charge of the burial poured quicklime on the body so that the remains would be destroyed." She further added: "Any medical or central file records of this man that we may have would have been destroyed as records are only kept a specified number of years after an inmate has died."

When all the records in the National Archives are open to the public, studied and scrutinized, such records will reveal that the electrocution of this man was a great miscarriage of justice.

Requiescat in Pace

58

WHITE EAGLETS GLIDE TO BETHLEHEM

Almost 2,000 years ago the dutiful children around *Gniezno*, Poland, returned to their homes in tears. They could not find any downy feathers of the white eaglets. The downy feathers were shed by the white eaglets around May 3rd, but here it was June, the seed planting completed, no school, but no downy feathers to be picked up at the base of the huge trees of the beautiful forests of Poland.

The parents pacified their children by inspecting the mammoth white eagle's nests. To their amazement, the downy feathers were hanging in bunches near the nests by an invisible thread. The ornithologists could not explain such "miracle" and they kept a vigilant eye on all the white eagles, eaglets, and the nests until December.

On the day before Christmas the heavenly skies were filled with the white eagles and eaglets, their strong beaks and tenacious talons gripped with the white down.

The eagles with their matured eaglets flew higher and higher until out of sight and into the air jet stream. Such jet stream has only been seen once in all of *Wielka Polska's* recorded mythology. The air jet stream glided the white eagles and the matured eaglets south to a warm climate, faster than the speed of light.

The southern town children and elders noticed the darkening evening skies suddenly becoming a brilliant gold and white, as all the white eagles were in the southern town with the white fluffy down. The soaring peaceful white eagles silenced the surrounding area where all the animals and people raised their eyes to heaven.

Suddenly all the busy silk worms came out of hibernation and finished their immaculate silk pillow cases that floated in the air.

The eagles filled all the pillows with the soft down. The pillows in their brilliance enlightened the skies which helped travellers reach home or their destination for Christmas, especially those travelling by donkey.

All of the animals were relaxed and peaceful as the white eaglets with the fluffy pillows in their talons swooped down and placed the pillows and feather-bedding in the stable's manger.

Then the white eagles departed and in the sky was a very brilliant star.

At the stable Baby Jesus was placed on these feather beds, pillows, and covered with a down comforter.

The surplus pillows were flown back by the white eagles to Poland and that is why the *pierzyna* (feather comforter) originated—so Baby Jesus would be comfortable and warm on Christmas Day.

Baby Jesus was lying in and covered with the soft down of the white eagle that was obtained from the white eaglets who transported their own baby down on their maiden flight. Returning to their huge nests towering the majestic forests the eaglets "sang" carols all Christmas day, the only time that the natives ever heard eagles sing.

59
THE INVISIBLE MIST MYSTERY

At 5:00 a.m. on Sunday, October 11, 1908, the Posen, Michigan area people were all awakened. The huge usually melodious church bells sounded mystically and one hour ahead of the usual 6:00 a.m. church bell ringing.

As in any rural area, the sounding at an odd hour of any church or school bell indicated a fire or a great tragedy.

Across the road from the church in Section nine, Frances (nee Pawlak) Wojtych Wekwert immediately arose.

Frances, then being 73 years of age, never witnessed such strange mystical sound of the bells. She was one of the first women homesteaders in 1870, when 160 acres of the virgin land was obtained for fourteen dollars.

Glancing across the road she witnessed the inside of the newly constructed church aglow with a pale-blue-silver light. That area had no electricity at that time of history.

Being robust and fearless all of her life, Frances walked toward the due north and south road. Escorted by her grandchildren, the group stopped when the organ music struck their attentative ears. The musical song was a Polish Church song, *Serdeczna Matko* (Sorrowful Mother).

Frances being very knowledgable due to her extensive reading, stated "Today is the feast day of the Mother of the Blessed Virgin Mother." She then quickly added, "It is also the anniversary day of the death of Casimer Pulaski at the Battle of Savanah".

The group then crossed the road and were joined by the priest, teaching nuns, the church sexton with his wife, and other persons from the immediate area.

The church sexton stated that the organist would not arrive until seven o'clock. He could not explain the bell ringing, lights in the church, and who was pumping the organ?

The area residents began arriving on horseback. There was complete silence by all after witnessing these unusual phenomena.

The ringing of the bells, the organ music and the lights in the church were quickly forgotten when an irritable, odorous western wind became almost unbearable, in gusting its almost invisible mist.

The sheep and the cattle in the pasture returned to the barns. The domestic ducks and geese left their ponds and streams, returning to the barn area. The birds in flight were heading due east for the shores of Lake Huron.

In that era of history, the sulfuric smell was related to the "fire of Hell".

A reference book utilized by Frances, who explained to the grandchildren that sulfur is a chemical and was discovered over three thousand years ago.

After the last church service, all of the people returned to their respective homes.

France's fortysix year old son-in-law upon completing the farm chores, stated that the sheep and cattle did not return to the pasture land. Even the farm horses would not eat their hay and grain.

Knowledgable of the Great Lakea area, Frances then said that the odor could have been the remains of a gigantic forest fire in the Minnesota or Wisconsin regions. However, she also stated that the sulfuric smell is an indication of fire to come, as related in the "Good Book."

The due west blowing wind continued with its odorous smell on Monday and Tuesday.

Wednesday morning the wind shifted to the north. At noon it shifted to the east. At supper time to the south. At midnight it was completely calm, as the hooting of the owls was distinctly heard.

Thursday morning there was no wind. Shortly after high-noon, an unusual cloud darkened the westward sky.

The Posen residents realized that in the distance was an uncontrollable forest fire. They began making preparations to evacuate as their area had a forest fire forty years earlier in 1868. Was this a repetition in a forty year cycle?

As many of the residents congregated on their open fields, many grouped on the east side of the present M-65 Highway, at the vacant land near the church.

Whether they prayed silently was never recorded. The grouped residents were greatly relieved when the wind switched to the south, southwest, sparing their community.

The next day it was learned that they were spared the destructive forest fire that annihilated the Metz, Michigan area, and caused the greatest tragedy in that part of Northeastern Michigan.

This story was told in a whispering tone of voice at many (a)wakes during the late 1920's and 1930's. The mystery of the ringing church bells, the mystery of the non-manned organ playing, and the phenomenon of the lighted-up church was never fully explained to the then young inquisitive mind of the writer.

Listening to the persons who witnessed and experienced the invisible sulfuric mist and their gratitude for the south, southwest wind of October 15, 1908, leaves no doubt in the writer's mind, that this was experienced by the rugged homesteaders, their children and grandchildren.

Can these mysterious phenomena be explained today, using the advanced knowledge of science, or will these rare events always be listed as unique occurrences?

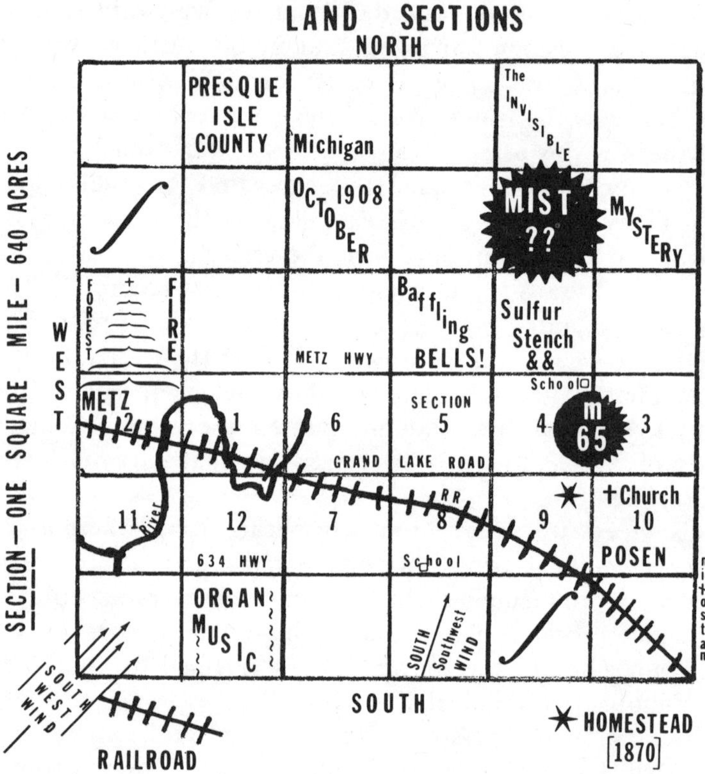
LAND SECTIONS
NORTH
SOUTH
WEST
EAST
SECTION—ONE SQUARE MILE—640 ACRES
PRESQUE ISLE COUNTY
Michigan
OCTOBER 1908
The INVISIBLE
MIST ??
MYSTERY
FOREST FIRE
Baffling BELLS!
Sulfur Stench &&
METZ HWY
School
METZ
2
1
6
SECTION 5
4
m 65
3
GRAND LAKE ROAD
RR
River
11
12
7
8
9
+Church 10
POSEN
634 HWY
School
ORGAN MUSIC
SOUTH Southwest WIND
mitostan
SOUTH WEST WIND
RAILROAD
HOMESTEAD [1870]

ABOUT THE AUTHOR

Natsolim is the pen name of Harry Milostan, Macomb County, Michigan, attorney.

Born in Northeastern Michigan, where his paternal great-grandmother homesteaded, Milostan received his preparatory education in the East. He was a feature article writer for the Michigan State News, M.S.U., where his B.A. was received under a Gunson scholarship and being employed as a finish carpenter. His J.D. was received at the University of Detroit. There he was the Editor of the Law Journal.

Pomology and acrology are hobbies of the author. He is pictured alongside a three-year-old peach tree whose rootstock originated in Poland. Milostan predicts that such Polish rootstock will be utilized on all peach trees in the Great Lakes Region, due to the rootstock's adaptation to the weather and its frost resistant durability.

MASSPAC Publishing Company
48855 North Gratiot Avenue
Mt. Clemens, Michigan, 48045

(Cut along dotted line)

ORDER FORM

Additional copies of *Enduring Poles* can be ordered on this convenient form.

___	Soft Cover Book(s) @ $4.95	___
___	Hard Cover Book(s) @ $7.95	___
	Michigan Sales Tax 4% (if applicable)	___
	Shipping and Handling	.55
	TOTAL	___

Send check or money order to:

MASSPAC PUBLISHING COMPANY
48855 North Gratiot Avenue
Mt. Clemens, Michigan 48045

PLEASE PRINT

NAME: ______________________

ADDRESS: ______________________

CITY: ______________________

STATE: ______________ ZIP: ________